GREAT ACROSTICS

GREAT
ACROSTICS

Martin Greif

Sterling Publishing Co., Inc. New York
A STERLING/MAIN STREET BOOK

Designed and Typeset by Sheila Kern, Cork, Ireland.

10   9   8   7   6   5   4   3   2   1

A Sterling/Main Street Book

Published in 1997 by Sterling Publishing Company, Inc.
387 Park Avenue South, New York, N.Y. 10016
© 1997 by Sterling Publishing Company, Inc.
Distributed in Canada by Sterling Publishing
c/o Canadian Manda Group, One Atlantic Avenue, Suite 105
Toronto, Ontario, Canada M6K 3E7
Distributed in Great Britain and Europe by Cassell PLC
Wellington House, 125 Strand, London WC2R 0BB, England
Distributed in Australia by Capricorn Link (Australia) Pty Ltd.
P.O. Box 6651, Baulkham Hills, Business Centre, NSW 2153, Australia

Manufactured in the United States of America

Sterling ISBN 0-8069-9471-1

Contents

Introduction

An acrostic is a series of words or lines of writing whose initial letter, taken in the order in which they stand, form a word or words, or some significant combinations of letters. Such a phenomenon will occasionally arise by accident, e.g. in the Fifth Aeneid Virgil writes:

Spicula caelatamque argento ferre bipennum;
Omnibus hic erit unus honos. Tres praemia primi
Accipient, flavaque caput nectentur oliva;
Primus equum phaleris insignem victor haneto.

If there was any reason to think that Virgil had been conversant with modern English, we might have looked around eagerly at the adjoining lines to find out what kind of soap he was advertising

It is almost impossible that a group of consecutive lines should form themselves into an acrostic of any length: partly because the law of averages comes in, partly because the chances are considerably against the occurrence of enough vowels to make the word formed by the initial sonant. The natural acrostic, therefore, does not occur, for practical purposes; if such a combination of letters presents itself to us in literature, we take it that it was put there on purpose.

Around the time of the 'sixties of the last century, and from some unknown source, the Acrostic Enigma burst on the world. The acrostic enigma (which, nowadays, we simply call an acrostic) does not set down in cold print the words of which the structure is composed. It refers to them by distant hints and far-fetched synonyms; the reader is expected to guess the words thus mystically indicated for himself. Take an easy example:

UPRIGHTS — TABLE TENNIS

Light 1. The father of Alexander the Great.
Light 2. Othello's ancient.
Light 3. The discovery of the laws of gravitation.
Light 4. A substitute for the dinner-bell.

For "table-tennis" you have to substitute "ping-pong"—it would be hard to find another synonym. That means that the four lights will be P...P, I...O, N...N, and G...G respectively. Nor is it difficult to identify Alexander's father with "Philip," Othello's ancient with "Iago," the discover of the laws of gravitation with "Newton," and the dinner-bell substitute with "gong." There is, no doubt, when the literary allusions become obscure, the phrasing ambiguous, the choice of synonyms complicated, that the art of the acrostic begins.

And what an art it is! For here you have the marriage of two minds, the composer's and the solver's, after many delays, false starts, misunderstandings. It is romance in miniature. Romance? A detective story more likely, with clues to guide you and clues to mislead you, with the gradual realization of the plot, the sudden gasp of recognition. Or, if you like, it is the duel between two brains, the quickness of the solver's lunge developing in answer to the deftness of the composer's parry.

A comparison of our own acrostic with those of the 1860's makes an interesting study. Not only because that former document recaptures a bygone historical atmosphere but because the acrostic itself has changed, and surely improved, with the times. One difference cannot fail to be noted: the previous composers had not learned to mutilate words, only using a fraction of a word as the light. This has its conveniences for construction: it is often impossible to make up a triple, still more a quadruple acrostic, without such truncation. Say, for example, you are constructing a quadruple acrostic, and the four letters you want are GLAM. The word that immediately occurs to you is "Glamorgan", but somehow how it must be docked to suit the editorial convenience. If you are writing for beginners, you merely say:

> The first four letters of a part of Wales

or (hardly less elementary)

> Let a musical instrument here
> From a country in Wales disappear.

But so far the process of abbreviation has only made things easier for the editor; it has not made things more difficult for the solver. This (though not difficult) would be an improvement:

> A county in Cambria's land
> (Unaccompanied here) we demand.

By this time, the cutting off of the last two syllables has ceased to be a mere *pis aller*; it has contributed to the mystery. Moreover, (and this is of exceptional importance), when the word "Glamorgan" does occur to the solver, he knows that he is right. He sees that Glamorgan is meant; he does not have to speculate.

This quality, of course, is what we allude to when we say that a particular light "clicks." A good light should, if possible, always carry with it its own guarantee of certainty. There should be one answer, and only one, that clearly satisfies the conditions; it may be as obscure as you like, but once you've got it you know you're there, and that further search is unnecessary. If I know (from the uprights, already guessed) that M-S are the two letters required, and read:

> A Roman general, famous for
> His exploits in the Punic War,

I may guess Metellus; but I may equally guess Marcellus or Maximus. But if I read:

> A great toxophilist inside
> This famous general is descried,

the light is harder to guess, as I have my choice between all the generals of history. But once I have thought of Metellus, I see the letters TELL inside him, and know that I have got the right solution.

To set about tackling an acrostic I can offer some advice. As a general rule, find all the lights that can be discovered with certainty, and then, using these for leverage, spend a quiet hour with the uprights, determined to solve them. Once you have found a plausible suggestion for these, read through the light again and see if any more of them fit; if you cannot find any, look for a new pair of uprights. In his study the solver has close to his elbow a bookcase, stocked with all the necessary tools of his craft. The Bible will be there, and Cruden (who went mad, they say, writing his Concordance), Shakespeare, and Cowden Clarke if you have it; no other poets, except perhaps Tennyson and an Oxford Book or Golden Treasury. Dictionaries you must have – encyclopedias are too bulky.

I must add a word or two about the rules which I have observed in writing the specimen acrostics which follow. They are doubtless acrostics, except where otherwise stated: each light, except where it is otherwise stated, consists of a single word, or a collection of words, typographically distinct from the other. Triple, quadruple and quintuple acrostics are accurately spaced, so that each significant letter in a given light is separated from the next by a uniform number of letters. For the pedantically accurate spelling of proper names I cannot answer; Biblical names are given in the form in which they appear in the Jacobean Bible, though in all but (I think) two cases the Douay Version may be used equally well; classical names are spelt in the Latin manner (Plato, not Platon). The puns which I have been fortunate enough to include are, for the most part, to be read by the eye, though one or two rather obvious ones are to be read by the ear.

With the numerical index of the uprights, by themselves, I have given the reader complete apparatus for finding out any solutions which he resolves to give up, if he finds them too difficult, and yet exercise his ingenuity in solving the lights. The lights are given in a second index, alphabetically arranged.

What is the future of the acrostic? Some have feared that all the possible uprights and all the possible lights will in time be used up; but this probability seems remote, and one might argue the same about (for example) the future of music. No art can die wholly; somewhere in the quiet corners of our minds the flame will be fanned and we shall return to the acrostic.

I

UPRIGHTS

A. "When shall their glory fade?
   O, the wild charge they made!"
B.   "... Shall ne'er go by
   From this day to the ending of the world,
   But we in it shall be remembered,
   We few, we happy few, we band of brothers."

LIGHTS

1. Queen in England, suggesting at a glance
   A kind of serpent and a game of chance.

2. From a collected total you subtract
   Goddess of vengeance (Greek, to be exact).

3. Helps you with your Greek: omit
   What (I hope) you do to it.

4. For another name for England you must rummage
   (Quite easy, if you've a friend living at West Bromwich).

5. An acid kind of person, or a kind of acid thing, which
   By the order of the letters you must carefully distinguish.

6. African river: you'd expect to find
   The relics of a Pontiff there enshrined.

7. Men who lack this as stupid we condemn;
   It gets its own back here by lacking them.

8. When bored, Sherlock Holmes would this monogram
      scrawl
   In revolver-shots over the opposite wall.

9. Take a letter away from a lady you know,
   And you've got nothing more than an insect to show.

II

UPRIGHTS

A famous author, known not least
For his acquaintance with the East.

LIGHTS

1. Strike it, and lo!
   Down you go.

2. One at each English batsman's end appears
   (Cut off the Royal Engineers).

3. You feel this, when the voice of Hope is dumb:
   Here, you reduce it to a vacuum.

4. Kind of noise
   Made by boys.

5. This word is rather queer:
   It means a Zulu spear.

6. He put his brother in a pit,
   And vainly searched for him in it.

7. A kind of tooth I here disclose,
   Of watch, of whip, of ma, of rose.

III

UPRIGHTS

A and *B*. Not this, but that—famous remark
Made by a punning hierarch.

LIGHTS

1. The land whence they came
Had a king, of what name?

2. What people invaded
England after they did?

3. And now for the first letters (four)
Of the name which the hierarch bore.

4. He wanted and got
These poor folk to do what?

5. Remote from this curse
(Which is just the reverse).

6. The companions in fight
Of my former upright.

IV

UPRIGHTS

A and *B*. You knocked the man down in a fight?
Then you're guilty of either upright.

LIGHTS

1. Rash was this king the prophet to neglect,
   Reversed, a prophet, but of curious sect.

2. Its queen was overcome with admiration,
   Reversed, a Gallic cry of execration.

3. A kind or species of thing,
   Reversed, an early Trojan king.

4. Find what translates this word in Latin, or,
   Reversed, "thy goods" (in Latin as before).

5. "What earthly this are snails?" you theorize,
   Reversed, "To eat!" the *chef* in Latin cries.

6. A description that's apt to be taken amiss,
   Reversed, if you use it, you're thought to do this.

7. A prominent river well known to the Scot,
   Reverse, Symons had one—though heaven knows what!

V

UPRIGHTS

A and *B*. On this, or on that were you bent,
When last up to London you went?

LIGHTS

1. A cake with a curious name
   From a country well known for the same.

2. In the humblest of flowers there is
   (As you might have expected) there's this.

3. Still more to come?
   Yes, here is some.

4. This beast, were its head in its tum,
   Would once a British Dominion become.

5. In nouns that are concrete, this end
   Would a cape or projection portend.

6. His fortunes he couldn't recoup
   After paying too dear for his soup.

7. Unfelt and unseen it has passed,
   Though it may be unerringly cast.

8. Rather like Number Three—one might claim
   That it is, yet it isn't the same.

VI

UPRIGHTS

A and *B*. Diamonds *here* untold,
And *there* uncounted gold.

LIGHTS

1. You might expect to hear this bird complain.
   The owl? The nightingale? No, guess again.
2. A College has this name,
   A window has the same.
3. Of times remote a narrative untrue;
   Reminds me of a foot, doesn't it you?
4. This word, I believe (I put that in
   On purpose), is properly Latin.
5. Right in the midst of this tree
   A point of the compass you'll see.
6. Sickness at which one's heartless comrades laugh
   When it's occasioned by its latter half.
7. Adding three letters, you'll
   Make a slough of a pool.
8. It forms the end of No. 2 Upright;
   And so without it you can do this light.

VII

Uprights

A. Your calculation false will be
   If the point you fail to see.
B. Part of this you mustn't waste
   For the rest comes on with haste.
A and B. Together, did the English get
   The thing in Albion yet?

Lights

1. A man of this temper deserves to be shot;
   If you aim at the middle, you're right on the spot.
2. Put this on a commodity—'twill call
   Out the reverse of this to great and small.
3. One of the States you'll emend,
   Doing itself to its end.
4. How strange that in this creature there should be
   An echo of Gregorian melody!
5. A man of this a Saint did seem
   To converse with in a dream.
6. "The bitterness of death is passed"—the worst
   Was over, since he was himself reversed.
7. Generous? Yes;
   Simply S.

VIII

UPRIGHTS

A and *B*. Two English regiments.

LIGHTS

1. A person, or a bay—
   You hear it, or you wear:
   Combine the two—it may
   Protect you from the air.

2. A German river, I admit;
   Yet you won't find Cologne on it.

3. Add pace to flimsy wear
   And you will find it tear.

4. A hill, or fluff—
   There, that's enough.

5. Yearly this day comes round, and spares
   Nor age nor sex (its name declares).

6. Some rivers have facilities
   For bathing—you can dress in this.

7. An alchemist—remove (not rightly spelled)
   Feeling by energetic people felt.

8. Heavenly marvel; its inside
   They may wear who push-bikes ride.

9. Fierce passion, turning, many a town,
   Nay, even kingdoms upside down.

10. My goodness! there's a maid
    In the treacle, I'm afraid.

IX

UPRIGHTS

A and *B.* This Acrostic kindly do
In the shape of Upright Two—
A building in a land of sun
Raised long since by Upright One.

LIGHTS

1. Soft and low
   Let the music go.

2. A kind of boat; if you should add a cave
   You'd find that she would often misbehave.

3. This ancient Gallic river when you've found
   You've got a Yankee war-cry wrong way round.

4. A heroine Meredithian; her
   Surname suggests a foreigner

5. His protest in enigmas let us sing—
   WB opens check upon RK.

6. A Grecian people bring to mind—
   The name contains a pun, you'll find.

7. A lovely spot in England. What a bore!
   The head comes last, the latter part before.

X

SOME SHAKESPEARE CHARACTERS

Uprights

A. A heroine's surname, ending with the same
Two letters as her well-known Christian name.
B. His father had three boys: one you must guess,
Who bore the same name in Italian dress.

Lights

1. He caused unnecessary grief
By finding some one's handkerchief.

2. His death resulted from a fall
Sustained in leaping from a wall.

3. A modern weapon though he brings to mind,
His place among the ancients you will find.

4. Most heroines had their handmaidens, but one
Hero this lady's service did not shun.

5. A bishop, who, upsetting everything,
Gave welcome counsel to a doubtful king.

6. Surprised apparently (but he knew better!)
By his own father looking at a letter.

7. Who first said, "Misery acquaints a man
With strange bedfellows" when the storm began?

XI

MORE SHAKESPEARE CHARACTERS

UPRIGHTS

(A) the orphan and *(B)* the intended victim of fratricide.

LIGHTS

1. Off, while she slept, her faithless lover went
   With her acrostical equivalent.

2. For twelve long years, through foe's design,
   Condemned (in every sense) to pine.

3. Pythagoras' philosophy
   Did not command his sympathy.

4. He made a damsel go
   By merely saying "Oh!"

5. Nobly he dared to disobey
   His master, when he turned away.

6. He sensibly declined to fight
   Over a girl who loathed his sight.

XII

UPRIGHTS

A and *B*. Unless you're having this for that each day,
You're dining in a most un-English way.

LIGHTS

1. An heir to King Solomon's crown
   Once left this East African town.
2. A wicked beast, although its function true
   Seems to be what we make all schoolboys do.
3. This word some lexicons don't give
   But rather its comparative.
4. This island makes
   No room for snakes.
5. The steeple-jack on chimney-pot,
   He * an awful lot.
6. Few words of mine a Bowdler would exscind
   But this one's sailing rather near the wind.
7. This Indian town please comprehend
   Before it has an evil end.
8. A tiny addition will make it the name
   Of a goddess who brings us to glory or shame.
9. Existed once, but doesn't at this minute:—
   A pity, too, because there's money in it.

XIII

UPRIGHTS

A and *B*. Familiar names
Of once popular children's games.

LIGHTS

1. The fragrant name is here
   Of ox or rat or deer.

2. Unwearied, this light.
   Ring off: that's all right.

3. Without it means
   In Shakespeare's scenes.

4. Twice one in mathematics? "Two." Good shot!
   Twice one in ornithology is—what?

5. Italian known to fame—
   Welcome his Christian name.

6. Rain, hail, snow, wind
   There you won't find.

7. Biblical Criticism's what this man did;
   Some think he was a trifle heavy-handed.

8. Something in London Town I am,
   Of Eton chap the anagram.

9. Grecian deity a Tom
   By one letter differs from.

10. Slightly open; potentate
    (When reversed) 'twill indicate.

11. American State: on four letters insist,
    But when you are just in the middle, then hist!

12. A boy of the kind you see here
    At a crumpet might easily jeer.

13. Title of Neptune; find it out
    By itself, to leave no doubt.

XIV

UPRIGHTS

Two names–a bird and a rhyme to one:
Great things for England each has done.

LIGHTS

1. A fish discover first,
   Better left unreversed.

2. You're doing this, if (lost to courtesy)
   Its own reverse you shout at somebody.

3. Painful disorder; shell it like a pea,
   And the result an Indian town you'll see.

4. Stares men in the face
   When exposure takes place.

5. This, or something like it, may
   The belated traveler say;
   But the bus has gone away.

XV

TRIPLE ACROSTIC

UPRIGHTS

Three names—two birds, and a rhyme to one:
Great deeds for England each has done.

LIGHTS

1. Humanitarian she
   Had not the means to be.

2. One woman, in those numerous tomes,
   Outwitted Mr. Sherlock Holmes.

3. Home of a language that is pure romance–
   Not Portugal, Spain, Italy, or France.

4. Curious, this designation
   Of a curious organization.

5. —— !

XVI

QUADRUPLE ACROSTIC

UPRIGHTS

Four names—three birds and a rhyme to one:
Great things for England each has done.

LIGHTS

1. She sang a song.
   Obscure and long.

2. The patriot's favorite investment find:
   Behead, behead, curtail—what's left behind?

3. A stone, yet made of wood? Turn it about,
   And leave the Latin-French conjunction out.

4. The much-stammered name
   Of an unattached dame.

5. Synonym for
   Expositor.

XVII

TRIPLE ACROSTIC

UPRIGHTS

A, *B*, and *C*. Far away, out of touch, out of sight,
out of speech,
This threefold connection its object can
reach.

LIGHTS

1. This verb can try you highly, when you are
Pronouncing it in second singular.

2. Existence is a bore—
Combined with this, still more.

3. This adjective would mean some learned College
Recognized limpets as a branch of knowledge.

4. Not quite so cordial as it might have been—
(Part of the Scriptures twice must intervene).

5. Alas, that rows of ugly mills
Disfigure, Derbyshire, thy hills!

6. When more attention Aviation's claimed,
An auto accident may thus be named.

7. Rash borrower! Very nearly he
Forfeited his security.

8. This fruit, unless a well-known story's feigned,
The makings of a vehicle contained.

9. "Infernal nuisance" who could call
This plant that's so medicinal?

XVIII

UPRIGHTS

A and *B*. Each bears a name that English patriot hearts
    can thrill:
    Each, noise, smoke, dirt, bustle and traffic
    fill.

LIGHTS

1. If you take it,
   You mustn't break it.

2. An army whose behavior signified
   The anger its initialled name implied.

3. A Roman–I hope you can find him,
   Although he's left nothing behind him.

4. A voice in your ear
   When there's nobody near.

5. This light contains no mysteries;
   Either it isn't, or it is.

6. What is made by a baker
   Or done by a breaker.

7. What a curious thought—if you recognize this,
   It is what it ain't, and it ain't what it is!

8. Not a prayer, nor an oath,
   And yet it means both.

XIX

UPRIGHTS

A and *B*. Two gentlemen who hit upon a plan,
And ask you to conceive them if you can.

LIGHTS

1. The name that schoolboys give to what they eat,
And that of an imaginary street.

2. The noble savage well he loved,
But he'd have known much better,
If C before his name were shoved
As its initial letter.

3. To public performers when this we accord,
It doesn't mean eggs on the platform are poured.

4. A stretch of usually tranquil wave,
But when you're *in* it, Lord, how people rave!

5. Had this been applied to it, surely the touch
Of a hand wouldn't quite be regretted so much.

6. Leave L out from a Scottish chieftain's name,
And you will find it answers just the same.

7. Is it in earth or sky?
It's neither, I reply.

8. A royal name: to half of it you might
Find many an ordinary man who has a right.

9. It's given to foe, but not to friend,
And has a very painful end.

XX

UPRIGHTS

A and *B*. Pedestrian undeterred
      Of whom we all once heard.

LIGHTS

1. A ponderous tome—might also be expected
   With the strange word SEVOLC to be connected.

2. Fat—but you'll miss
   The point of this.

3. A great relief—but then it's true
   We'd been unlucky hitherto.

4. Not quite a Paradise, though 'twas regained,
   And, you may say, a Paradise contained.

5. The days of Lent
   'Twill represent.

6. Known by the poet's pen, but for
   The artist's pencil known still more.

7. A kind of space, from which it's to be feared
   A dignitary must have disappeared.

8. Part of a foot—inside
   A flower may be descried.

9. What's the name of it? Oh
   Confound it, *you* know.

XXI

UPRIGHTS

A and *B*. Two English actors of the past.

LIGHTS

1. Paternal sport will bring
   His furry covering:
   A bird or flag's the thing.

2. A constellation—or
   Comprised in No. 4.

3. Its middle is before—name for a hound,
   Or of a speaker with less sense than sound.

4. Finance controller, who
   Comprises No. 2.

5. Thoroughly stupid, you rightly divine,—
   You must leave it three letters by cutting off nine.

6. Got the first half? Of course! Meanwhile
   The whole is an artistic style.

7. A special sum to allocate
   For purposes you contemplate.

XXII

UPRIGHTS

Two counties by the brine,
Once reached by the Great Western Line.

LIGHTS

1. A race which Nature did design
   For commerce (features aquiline).

2. To find it, you will have to go
   Some hundred miles from Buffalo.

3. He finishes off the poor beast
   When the crowd from its blood-lust has ceased.

4. Full many a goose ere now has been
   This in this school, as I have seen.

5. It means you look through it again;
   But don't let the city remain.

6. With stretch how vast to either hand
   We see it yawn on Afric's strand!

7. Problem of conduct, hard to explicate;
   Alas! still harder to eradicate.

8. On the fruits which this can give
   Must the proletariat live

XXIII

UPRIGHTS

A and *B*. These two, they say,
  All priests obey.

LIGHTS

1. It grows in the garden; but there is the riddle—
   It's a center inside which is not in the middle!

2. Central African name, which (of course)
   One might also address to a horse.

3. The fault, dear . . . , is not in our stars
   But in ourselves.

4. Half one upright, and all but a third
   Of the other, you tell me? Absurd!

5. Nice buildings, Jones, you do!
   I enter them, say you.

6. It must be more than one, but not too many.
   The curious thing is, here there isn't any.

XXIV

UPRIGHTS

A and *B* (in one). Until recently the name of a European nation—
Or should we say amalgamation?

LIGHTS

1. Surely this weapon can't have been designed
   Only to mangle helpless womankind?

2. His Jewish fellow-countrymen
   Offered a subject for his pen.

3. It suggests a conclusion—reverse it, it means
   A person encountered in climbing up beans.

4. On the hill-side a flaw
   (Presupposing a thaw).

5. Take the last of the lot, and for him do your best,
   Advancing him over the heads of the rest.

6. This light
   Is quite
   All right.

XXV

UPRIGHTS

A. Though often told one day my feet I'd set
   Upon this road, I've never been there yet.
B. I wonder, could they have been meaning *here*?
   Its inmates hustle, but they're also queer.

LIGHTS

1. "To whom did my boy George —— else?"

2. "Let not Ambition mock their —— toil."

3. "The lily maid of Astolat."

4. "Great praise the Duke of Marlborough won,
       And our good Prince —— "

5. "Strew on her roses, roses."

6. "And there were gardens bright with —— rills."

7. "From his glacier cold, with his —— the mountains
       strook."

8. "See where this —— comes me cranking in."

9. "Stout Cortes, when with —— eyes He stared at the
       Pacific."

10. "He seemed to be, Not one, but all mankind's ——"

11. "Oh, that the present hour would lend Another —— of
        the kind!"

XXVI

Uprights

"Bluish 'mid the burning water, full in face . . . lay:
In the dimmest North-east distance dawned. . .
grand and grey."

Lights

1. " . . . the accomplishment of many years
Into an hour-glass."

2. " . . . Ben Levi on the Sabbath read
A volume of the Law."

3. "For of . . ., prince of Tartary, I sing."

4. "The weariness, the . . ., and the fret,
Here where men sit, and hear each other groan."

5. " . . . arose from her couch of snows."

6. "And drowsy tinklings . . . the distant folds."

7. "And . . . in being old."

8.   "From her post
Of purview at a window, languidly
A great . . . watched his Collieship."

9. "And there lay the . . ., distorted and pale."

XXVII

AN ANAGRAMMATIC ACROSTIC

UPRIGHTS

A. Something to eat.
B. Its anagram—something to drive.

LIGHTS

1. Anagram of CHENILLE.

2. . . . . A ROUGH PAT.

3. . . . . EAR-CLIP.

4. . . . . NICER RATION.

5. . . . . REAL CHOIR.

6. . . . . ORATION.

7. . . . . ONE TANTRUM.

XXVIII

AN ANAGRAMMATICAL ACROSTIC

UPRIGHTS

A and *B*. Their difference in logic is obscure:
This against that it's better to insure.

LIGHTS

1. Anagram of PIRATED; a heroine.

2. . . . . CHARITEUM; a complaint.

3. . . . . RECIDOR; a chronicler.

4. . . . . IRISH CAP; a French author.

5. . . . . LANGDEN; something we are all
fond of.

6. . . . . A RAG TUNE; an undesirable.

7. . . . . TAINT; a monster.

8. . . . . GUSTY ONE; Mother's darling.

XXIX

AN ACROSTIC OF CHARADES

UPRIGHTS

A and *B*. A part of the Cheviots appears to reveal
The immediate result of the Corn Law
Repeal.

LIGHTS

1. Level my first, my second soon blows over;
   My whole oft loses more than he'll recover.

2. My first is before, and my second quite small
   My whole doesn't live with his fellows at all.

3. One half may get cold, but the other half? Nay!
   Smooth, brittle, and white, my poor whole's thrown
   away.

4. My second half runs o'er my first; my whole
   A bird whose raucous cries o'er marshes roll.

XXX

UPRIGHTS

A and *B*. Either upright has four feet.

LIGHTS

1. Whence named this missile? From some Roman's fling,
   Whose doubtful aim set people wondering?
2. A wayward spirit's name—if verb it were,
   The act of a bad sailor 'twould declare.
3. Combine we here a master of creation
   With creature that affords us education;
   And oh, how hard will be the combination!
4. A respectable lady, and yet
   She seems to invite us to bet.
5. A fish, or a serpent, and in it is shown
   An imperial city that's turned upside down.
6. Reproach—but cut away
   The trimmings, I should say.
7. This is a lively interlude,
   Yet all within is quietude.
8. Food, but who would wish
   To preserve the dish?
9. Animal and fruit combined—
   A comic watchman you will find.

XXXI

UPRIGHTS

A and *B*. Why must the English to alien countries fly,
When there's a substitute close by?

LIGHTS

1. Let us hope we shall find it, when death's drawing near,
Undiminished by what it's diminished by here.

2. Tax that's meant to regulate
Imports at the city gate.

3. Return to scenes of childish memories—
Is it superfluous? Of course it is.

4. Of an Italian city the new name
(Though it was always much the same).

5. To hint what's to someone's discredit—
Adam to Eve might have said it.

6. A very useful trade he plies—
Vindictive, if beheaded twice.

7. It seems to have been quite
An epoch-making flight.

XXXII

UPRIGHTS

A or *B*. A pastime much written about.

B or *A*. A thing you can't do it without.

LIGHTS

1. A burglar often uses it:
   Reversed, he often loses it.

2. A longish bit of history:
   Reversed, part of the verb to be.

3. A time you'll see no more:
   Reversed, describes a score.

4. After it you walk, no doubt:
   Turn it either way about.

5. In Latin you'll find it will go;
   Reversed—it's a pronoun you know.

6. What you feel when your fates are not soft;
   Reversed, he's the culprit full oft.

7. A kind, I think, of legal claim:
   Reversed, a Scottish Christian name.

8. A place that is somewhere in Scotland, I know;
   Reversed, it's a woman you loved long ago.

9. The address of a cockney demanding your reasons to
   hear;
   Reversed, it's an isle—add one letter, a State will
   appear.

10. These grandmamma full often takes,
    For a short (light reversed)—then wakes.

XXXIII

UPRIGHTS

A. Takes from an alien fruit its name untrue,
  And from a tree whereon it never grew.
B. Sunwards it turns, and thence acquired the name
  Which made men think from holy shores it came.

LIGHTS

1. Here many a hat
  'Neath the water they plait.

2. Talk between two
  Shut off from view.

3. "Dawning"; behead—"a climb"; behead once more—
  "A smell"; behead again— "a trifling store."

4. If you have done acrostics much before,
  This light you'll more than ever find a bore.

5. An insect, a bow, and a pain you'll find
  Into a distant sea combined.

6. Masonry true and tried,
  Yet it's got lint inside.

7. Has eyes, yet does not see,
  Buried in earth must be.

8. A thing you may cut any time,
  But to pick it is often a crime.

9. It keeps the schoolboy in from play,
  Or takes him out on muddy day.

XXXIV

UPRIGHTS

A and *B*. 'Twixt 98 and 37 you see
　　　A difference? It's a difference of degree.

LIGHTS

1. Word in fairly common use
　Simile to introduce.

2. Forceful personalities
　Frequently are held in this.

3. Different breeds this bird has got;
　One is called the Y.

4. "Bosh!" you say, or scent (perplexed)
　Some corruption in the text.

5. Hearing of his country's wreck,
　Down he fell and broke his neck.

6. Here's what women sometimes do—
　Men about it may do you.

7. Find in the accusative
　One who could through ages live.

8. Persons working on the stage
　Usually scan its page.

9. Here's a country far away,
　Not so distant as Cathay.

10. Men, whatever their degree,
　End in this extremity.

XXXV

UPRIGHTS

A and B. A philosophy don and his pupil please name
Number Two on the banks of a river won
   fame,
Which sounds like the Isis, but isn't the
   same.

LIGHTS

1. Purer than Jordan did the waters seem
   Of this, an obviously fruitful stream.

2. This orgy, turned round the wrong way,
   Will move an obstruction away.

3. Feigned name of English poet's sweetheart see—
   Politeness would have put it "Thou and me."

4. A famous Oxford don his brain might tax
   How to distinguish this from wheeling sacks.

5. Apparently inebriated song
   Sir Lancelot sang the river banks along.

6. A theologian—little difference we
   Between his name and origin shall see.

7. This word, let it mean what it may,
   Is something you do to your hay.

8. What, Ethel, by this stream perplexed?
   Why, you'll forget your own name next!

9. Take a clan from a month, and you'll find
   You've left nothing but ashes behind.

XXXVI

Uprights

A and *B*. Two formidable animals.

Lights

1. This was a king who "swore a royal oath,"
   And plighted (somewhat suddenly) his troth.

2. Fit for a king! A drink you might call this—
   Reverse the light to find out what it is.

3. Robbed of its tail, this bird with plumage gay
   Into a river vanishes away.

4. Ask him his views on politics to state,
   Nor be surprised to find him out of date.

5. This monarch may convince us, if we will,
   A giant halved can be a giant still.

6. Alas! This opera-singer does but need
   Inversion to convince us of her greed.

7. This is a singularly easy light;
   You've but to look at it to get it right.

8. Spite of appearances, you cannot claim
   This kind of shed has an Italian name.

9. The name of a musician you must seek,
   Partly (I'll tell you) Spanish, partly Greek.

XXXVII

TRIPLE ACROSTIC

UPRIGHTS

A, B, and C. Youth, beauty, and age,
   Portrayed on the stage.

LIGHTS

1. Strange home, in which Mamma's compelled to stay,
   Though all the young ones can run out and play.

2. Medicinal stuff—from foes of Israel's race
   The name appears its origin to trace.

3. Whose the beast from its conclusion takes
   Will find the man who this disturbance makes.

4. Take her away—what right had he
   To forfeit his celibacy?

5. Part of Portugal you choose,
   Or its three middle letters use.

6. Of or belonging to an argument
   On subjects chosen by the arguent.

7. "To-day the Roman and his trouble
      Are ashes under *this*"—
   That's from the *Shropshire Lad*; you will
      Its final letter miss.

8. Heroine, whose name
   Knowledge seems to claim.

9. He comes from a land
   Where the fishing is grand.

XXXVIII

QUADRUPLE ACROSTIC

Uprights

"Since there's no A, B, let us C and D."

Lights

1. Reverse the name a schoolboy might apply
   (For briefness) to his weekly subsidy.

2. A lady thus (but with an S)
   In Southern lands you might address.

3. Initials seen on many a truck.

4. To cattle-breeders brings bad luck.

XXXIX

QUADRUPLE ACROSTIC

UPRIGHTS

A. A tutelary deity.
B. Of stream, *C*, of mountain, *D*, or of tree.

LIGHTS

1. Some glittering things are *this* (get clear
   Your notions on Obversion here).

2. Wordsworthian stream! Thy peaceful flow
   Must banish every sound of woe.

3. As who should say
   "In a splendid way."

4. A frontier town, disputed without rest
   By anagrams of "hasten" and "behest."

5. Thus might we Argus with his numerous eyes
   Describe—or shall we say, apostrophize?

XL

QUADRUPLE ACROSTIC

Uprights

A, *B*, *C* and *D*. Four Roman statesmen.

Lights

1. Belonging to the official who amerced
   Dealers importing cattle in the first
   Century into Egypt. It's reversed.

2. On the East Coast of Scotland look for this;
   Here, its first letter be prepared to miss.

3. What brine may do to Channel swimmers' lips,
   Dirt to old coins, or barnacles to ships.

4. Though bright the radiant colors of its hope,
   This instrument suffers from lack of scope.

5. A river rolling on, with muddy tide,
   Through scenes of the Bellocian country-side.

6. What did the daisies look like, after Maud
   Had just passed through them, wandering abroad?

XLI

(Only seven different letters of the alphabet are to be used in solving this Acrostic.)

UPRIGHTS

A. This word is used to designate
   A very thin but solid plate.
B. And this description's one we share
   With cat and dog and wolf and bear.

LIGHTS

1. She hatched the trouble long before
   Which brought about the Trojan War.

2. His middle name was Breck, but here
   Let his true Christian name appear.

3. An Eastern folk, who didn't feel
   The slightest instinct for repeal.

4. And when you have reversed that name
   The word you'll find is just the same.

5. Mahabharata hero—yes,
   That is the name, I must confess.

6. Let Number One suggest a town,
   Then write a suburb of it down.

XLII

Uprights

A and *B*. Familiar processes, that long ago
　　Brought pain to almost everyone I know—
　　For every family on our poor earth
　　B will be found in death, and A in birth.

Lights

1. Your first impression throws much light,
   And is (I need not say) quite right.
2. His health is frail? Then I should say
   You'd better take the sweet away.
3. See where, our only refuge, hangs the boat!
   Cut it away, and let it safely float.
4. A Zulu army, not (I greatly fear)
   Of morals such as schoolboys would revere.
5. It says that they are bad,
   But, Lord! what them we've had!
6. See, far above those rainbow colors glow,
   Lacking the means to visit us below.
7. From Continental shores this bishop came,
   And brought with him a most inviting name.
8. Now, have a shot! Singular noun one sees
   With which a plural adjective agrees.

XLIII

UPRIGHTS

Could aught enhance the fame of B,
'Twas A that did it—who was he?
What! B's identity you doubt?
Then take your dictionary out.

LIGHTS

1. Small tribe of an easterly nation
   (Please submit it to examination).

2. A spot on a heel,
   That's touched a good deal.

3. What kind of bath is best
   For one who needs a rest?

4. For frailty a grim
   But exact synonym.

5. Not a bird after all
   But a way from the hall.

6. It runs to and fro with a squall
   Without any motive at all.

7. His son-in-law thrice served him well.
   Reversed, his widow married well.

XLIV

TRIPLE ACROSTIC

UPRIGHTS

A, B, and *C.* Three characters from Milton.

LIGHTS

1. Proverbially he
   Love's laughing-stock may be.
2. The name you may guess
   Of an Italian princess.
3. A Caledonian missile,
   The largest used in this British isle.
4. The ancient appellation see
   Of Terni and of Termini.
5. It gives a light
   (Though small) at night;
   A healthy way
   To start the day.
6. Stomach or thigh
   Headless we'll try.
7. An Eastern island far away;
   "I am black," it seems to say.

XLV

UPRIGHTS

A and *B*. Two English ranges of hills.

LIGHTS

1. Add 99 to 104—
   A spirit of which we should like to see more.
2. Shakespearean character—a rat we smell
   Between an English and a Latin yell.
3. An oxymoron, if the solver's this!
   Yet he may be so, if the prize he miss.
4. This beneath the earth should be;
   Its reverse, upon the sea.
5. What probably I
   Shall not exclaim as I die.
6. We smell another, in the name
   Of a Parnassus-haunting dame.
7. This to his fellow-men its own reverse
   Does, for he suffers from a loathsome curse.
8. This oft I've done when listening
   To its reverse a-lecturing.
9. This gem's third letter dropped, you will have found
   A lexicographer the wrong way round.

XLVI

TRIPLE ACROSTIC

UPRIGHTS

A, B, and *C.* Three English public schools.

LIGHTS

1. A place in County Cork you'll track—
   Wouldn't it be nice if its rector were black?
2. Unshortened name of well-known Christian feast,
   Not like a Jaffa orange in the least.
3. As down the Rhine you float
   This Siren-rock you note.
4. The name of the surgeon's assistant at sea
   Is this kind of boy (the last letter must flee).
5. As this the winter wind
   Is never so unkind.
6. Marshal, of lot accursed,
   Or Chinese coin reversed.
7. A fire reflected in a looking-glass?
   Rather obscure, that light, but let it pass.
8. This town in Scotland's far extremities
   (Without a railway sorting-office) lies.
9. This implement's wooden; from plank you will chop
   One-fifth at the bottom, one-fifth at the top.
10. Insipid and affected sort of stuff—
    Half of it, thank you, will be quite enough.

XLVII

A SONNET-ACROSTIC

UPRIGHTS

Two Poets on the Sonnet.

A. "A sonnet is a ——'s ——."

B.   " . . . When a damp
    Fell round the path of Milton, in his hands
    The thing——"

LIGHTS

1. She ate the junkets, so the old wives said.

2. Strange, that this bird a halo does not wear!

3. Twelve hundred—or eleven, for all I care.

4. Removes its nightcap, yet leaves not its bed.

5. King of an Islamic state recalling Lerna's dread.

6. Save head and tail you will find nothing there.

7. Lived—was it at the Mangy Goat, or where?

8. A leopard is too large; try this instead.

9. Low, but contains a mountain upside down.

10. To these four letters, which no meaning grant,

11. Two thousand add—one of the sights of Town!

12. A gentleman from Africa you want.

13. Weak at first sight, yet having won renown.

14. A feat on horseback, or a kind of slant.

XLVIII

Uprights

A. Within this rests the English ship from stormy seas.
B. And within this the Limey shipman takes his ease.

Lights

1. Her story by a bard of old
   (Who doesn't signify) is told.
2. See islands fair,
   Of human traces bare.
3. A pick-me-up we thus might name;
   Back-ways or front, it's all the same.
4. Shepherdess
   In distress.
5. This instrument in Spain is made;
   Suggests Italian serenade.
6. A tradesman who for you exerts his skill,
   Yet somehow never sends you in a bill.
7. Mellivorous beast! What a mistake
   If we confused you with a snake!
8. Festive as we on this occasion are,
   It makes one think of "moaning at the bar."
9. From this metal (a curious fact)
   Red lead we shall try to extract.
10. A garment that sometimes is worn on the seas
    Is what I itself to with only two E's.

XLIX

UPRIGHTS

A and *B*. Two great battles between England and a
near neighbor.

LIGHTS

1. Lancashire town, whose name ensures
   Support—I hope it won't put yours!
2. When hot
   It's rot.
3. Not now, and certainly not here;
   Yet in a sense it's both—how queer!
4. May be a potentate
   Or may intoxicate.
5. Useful? Why, no; but here
   At least the name is clear.
6. A fortune you may lose or win in it.
   Dishonest? No; and yet there's sin in it.
7. Were this turned upside down by some young wag,
   We should see red, and we should see a rag.
8. Elam eht ffo tuc
   Professor from its tail.
9. He doesn't care, although his home's aflame,
   And he himself is here discovered lame.
10. Two important towns in old Palestine
    To make Mohammedans more thin combine.
11. Are we downhearted? Let the sigh
    Of southern breezes make reply!

L

Uprights

A. An English novelist.
B. A work by that novelist.

Lights

1. A bulwark of the English system see:
   One letter interpose, an alien he.

2. A goddess's name, but the curious part
   Is the fact that it doesn't begin at the start.

3. It's down below; behead,
       And it is up on high:
   It's neither, if instead
       You should insert an I.

4. Easily hidden? I should rather say
   The very air its presence doth betray.

5. Take from a charm what doesn't count, and write
   Three letters only, which make up the light.

6. Reverse those letters—Number Six I sing—
   Three-quarters of an ancient Roman king.

7. Poor soul! 'Mid poverty and dark despairs,
   Half of herself she sews, and half she tears.

8. Ninth king of Israel might
   Have been, but wasn't quite.

9. Could but this river backwards go, what fun,
   Scholars, that in a circle it should run!

10. In the course of an eight-letter word
    Three N's and three E's have occurred.

LI

UPRIGHTS

A and *B*. They dwelt beneath the greenwood tree,
The one providing clothes, you see,
The other food. (Weak pleasantry.)

LIGHTS

1. This piece of dress is now no more,
   Nor yet the bird (on British shore).
2. He wields the brush, but not the pen; so I
   Suspect there's been a lapsus calami.
3. Spanish-American this land you'll find—
   "Away, away!" cries the Italian mind.
4. "Able was I ere I saw *this*"—you know
   The riddle. What was *this* called, long ago?
5. Sectarian he, yet not, as you'd suppose,
   One of the Friends, so nicknamed by his foes.
6. A temperature, a number, a small glass—
   These form a race, of the Hamitic class.
7. "To Mr. So-and-so, or . . . "—what comes here?
   (The jetty, jettisoned, must disappear.)
8. One of the few survivors in a play
   Most of whose characters are done away.
9. By this ornithological name you may call
   The girl you're in love with, or nothing at all.

LII

TRIPLE ACROSTIC

UPRIGHTS

A, *B*, and *C*. A triad of poets; they're all of them dead;
    The first, from neglecting to cover his head;
    The second on fruit had incautiously fed
    The third came in pieces (or so it is said).

LIGHTS

1. Were killing no murder, one might feel inclined
   To do this to some people I've got in my mind.

2. This at least to the pedestrian there is nobody can do.
   You suggest, "Reverse the process"? well, I should if I
       were you.

3. The part's but a humble one he would apply for,
   Yet it's this kind of man some philosophers cry for.

4. They called themselves pure, and we hope that they
       were,
   But why to such secret assemblies repair?

5. This word is bound to scandalize—
   Dancing and drinking it implies.

6. Such a blast you'd expect from the North, I'll be bound,
   But here you will find it the other way round.

7. A distinction much prized; were it mine, I confess
   I'd prefer the last letter but one should be S.

8. Such was even the slightest clause
   Of the Medo-Persian laws.

9. A king of Egypt; I
   Forget what dynasty.

LIII

UPRIGHTS

Two Victorian novelists.

LIGHTS

1. While crowds disperse,
   It goes through its reverse.

2. It isn't true;
   It's just your fancy, Sue

3. Grows in a bed
   (A tradesman's lost his head).

4. Drop last and first,
   Her name is fête reversed.

5. Back to its shore
   The high road leads no more.

6. Let childless prayer
   Alternative declare.

7. Reverse a bit,
   And you can drive in it.

8. Precisely; this
   Of course is what it is.

LIV

TRIPLE ACROSTIC

UPRIGHTS

A, *B*, and *C*. Three Shakespeare heroines.

LIGHTS

1. Take from the theme of Aristotle's page
   Unfortunate French girl, of tender age,
   And nought is left you but a Jewish sage.

2. Three letters, by inserting which you may
   Make proper names of Tinson and of Brey.

3. When he dies, straightway
   That he may live we pray.

4. Reverse, when you've disabled (what an odd use
   Of terms!) this kind of market-garden produce.

5. Shy traffickers in bygone day
   With the Phoenician merchants they.

6. Name of a country here will win—
   An anagram of a great inn.

LV

UPRIGHTS

A and *B*. Two old musical instruments.

LIGHTS

1. This light's a simple one;
   You get it from the sun.

2. Name assigned to Sinaitic
   Manuscript by German critic.

3. Receptacle, removing (I'm afraid)
   From Greek philosopher his cry for aid.

4. A garment whose inside (that's wit)
   Explains that you are wearing it.

5. An obstacle, yet, strange to say,
   Its name implies it runs away.

6. Serbian town, yet it would seem
   More than half an English stream.

7. Something which a savage crew
   Mustn't say or mustn't do.

LVI

UPRIGHTS

A and *B*. Near Birmingham or Bristol find a name.
A. Part bears a sword, the other part a flame.
B. The order's different, but each part's the same.

LIGHTS

1. The second part of A (or first of B)
   Is dying down—a place in Ireland see.

2. The ancestor of Eastern tyrants he,
   Fatherless here himself, as you may see.

3. Poor fellow! 'Mid seas of false doctrine he's tossed;
   And I'm sorry to say you will find he is lost.

4. Strange creature, which can thus contain
   Three-fifths of its minute domain!

5. A poetess, whose gloomy turn of mind
   Might to her first four letters be assigned.

6. Dread country! There is frost in it;
   Thousands of lives were lost in it.

7. A bird—the picture of its former part,
   Signed by its latter, overjoys my heart.

LVII

UPRIGHTS

A and *B*. Two names, suggesting early 20th-century
luxury,
Or famous structures of antiquity.

LIGHTS

1. The glittering emblem of proud royalty
   Crumbles in smoke, alas! how rapidly.

2. This, shaped to represent nativity,
   Has witnessed century after century.

3. Nature her blessings with this kind of land
   Has showered, it seems, on almost every land.

4. A kind of native chieftain from the Southwest,
   Less dark, though, than his title would suggest.

5. Makes for the top, and scorns the depths below,
   Yet synonym for all the worst we know.

6. A kingly looking person he, and yet
   The prophet must decline him with regret.

7. Name of a color; but on cockney lips
   It means an English river, full of ships.

8. Heroine of poem of enormous size
   By author tedious as his name implies.

LVIII

UPRIGHTS

"Mortality, behold and fear!
What a change of dust is here!"

LIGHTS

1. Present and perfect of one verb employ,
   And find the means to "snatch a fearful joy."

2. Her wild lament protests
   That gone are both her brothers,
   Not (as her name suggests)
   Some sister of her mother's.

3. Pair wax their backs: sun shone—one gone!

4. A home that pays no rent
   And shuns advertisement.

5. It moves
   In grooves.

6. Field, where tyrranicide avenged must be
   And A victorious over B and C.

7. Welsh Christian name, which might suggest
   A church with chancel at the West.

8. Far-sighted as any could be,
   Yet more than short-sighted, was he.

9. If thou *this* an S, the mountain thou wilt guess.

10. Not knowing German, poor Lestrade
    Thought it referred to some fair maid.

11. An easy one, this,
    Which you really can't miss.

LIX

UPRIGHTS

A. The same as B.
B. The same as A.

LIGHTS

1. Same as the uprights.
2. Contains the promise either of life or of light.
3. The author's natural enemy.
4. Same as No. 1.
5. Another name for No. 3.
6. Same as No. 1.
7. Written by a Pope who was not infallible.
8. Same as No. 1.
9. Same as No. 2.
10. Same as No. 3.
11. Same as No. 1.

LX

UPRIGHTS

A and *B*. From this to that! Their country, with
small hurt,
Seemed to have staked on *rouge et noir* its
shirt.

LIGHTS

1. Fell in a glorious fray
Upon St. Crispin's Day.

2. A word of sadness—if its D were O,
It would provide a splendid vowel-show.

3. From this best take a cue;
It sees you safely through.

4. A light you cannot miss:
It does not do, but is.

5. All coachmen are fat men; some grooms are not fat;
Some grooms are not coachmen, then:—what mood
is that?

6. How would the name of it have differed
If it had not included Clifford?

7. A name of priestly origin,
And yet an anagram of sin.

8. For many a useful end employed,
And yet a thing all men avoid.

9. A crony: from his mate
He needs must separate.

LXI

UPRIGHTS

A and *B*. Two card games.

LIGHTS

1. A prison in a famous town,
   Which keeps a dragon upside down.

2. Where was a great Cathedral's varied art
   Sketched by a pilgrim from an apple-cart?

3. An ancient tongue—they called it so
   After the Sanskrit *jna*, "to know."

4. Consult, if more facts on the subject you'd know,
   The passage referred to a moment ago.

5. A beast like a horse—it will surely expire,
   With only one third of it clear of the mire!

6. Just a single verse, I fear,
   From the whole is missing here.

7. When a child plays at billiards, it learns it with—what?
   Combine it with something that rests on a pot,
   And an eminent mathematician you've got.

LXII

Uprights

A. Here the vast ocean heaves before our view,
And swarthy Ethiops for our favor sue.
B. Music o'er this hath such sweet potency
That even the name of it is poetry.

Lights

1. It is a license, I admit,
   To take away three-sevenths of it.
2. Forgetting quite what she was at,
   She left the Pope upon the mat.
3. Across the loch some Roman chieftain frowned
   And said that he would swim the wrong way round.
4. An answer to the question, "When did
   The Middle Ages find they'd ended?"
5. Disappeared by an underground route,
   And was afterwards traced by his boot.
6. When this across your lips you bring,
   Your thoughts will take some uttering.
7. A land that to a joker
   Might well suggest a stoker.
8. "Gad!" said the worshippers—the deity
   (Turned upside down) made suitable reply.
9. An island we refer to so—
   They don't call ours a ruby, though.

LXIII

UPRIGHTS

A and *B*. English places of pilgrimage
In a regretted age.

LIGHTS

1. This innocent fool
Is merely a tool.

2. Ramagna is itself of it. When found,
Reduce it by two-thousandths of a pound.

3. Whose troopers (a damnable lot)
The Cavalier gentleman shot?

4. He steered, without demanding any tip,
His famous comrades in a famous ship.

5. Just one word more, and that one word will prove
Short, if the Cardinal we should remove.

6. Transpose its two vowels—this gum
Has instantly higher become.

7. This boastfulness befits you, sir, no more
Than if you wore your clothes behind before.

8. Behead a Christian name;
What a disgusting shame!

9. How beautiful it is!
Is it a della this?

10. A plant in tropic climate born;
Reversed, a common English thorn.

LXIV

QUADRUPLE ACROSTIC
(The lights here are not single-word lights.)

UPRIGHTS

A and *B*. A religious work.
C and *D*. Another.

LIGHTS

1. This authoress once made shop-girls sob and gulp;
   I think her work is simply . . .
2. Granted these ceremonies boring are,
   You must admit one gets . . .
3. We lost the match (although we nearly drew)
   Just by a goal—a very . . .
4. True to his principles, this old sea-dog
   Nor sherry drinks, nor port, but . . .
5. Dante I've read: I seemed, as ne'er before,
   To hear the angels chant, the . . .
6. See, where she prays, remote from thoughts of ill,
   And all her world's nought but an . . .
7. On either side a yawning precipice
   Threatens destruction if we . . .
8. "Your father lives, *or no?*" The young *piou-piou*,
   Misunderstanding, said, "Il. . ."

LXV

UPRIGHTS

A and *B*. At this or in that
      My poor great-grandfather sat.

LIGHTS

1. For this you are put up, by this knocked down.
2. In this, Montgomery's an important town.
3. Nonsense; from back to front this hill you read.
4. In ecstasy, no torment does he heed.
5. Innocent this alarm; reversed, a bed.
6. That this to this succeeds, I've heard it said.
7. Reverse four-sevenths of Number Two: a lake.
8. Italian town; reverse, a heathen fake.
9. A dignitary takes his title thence:
    Reversed, it's part of his magnificence.

LXVI

UPRIGHTS

A and *B*. Two creatures you have often seen, I bet,
　　　　But neither of them with a head on yet.

LIGHTS

1. Is it gas? you cry.
   Quite the reverse, say I.

2. This *is* a gas, suggesting at a glance
   One of the theaters of war in France.

3. Classical work, whose estimation
   Is proved by frequent itselfation.

4. Presumably the thing I mean
   (If it's in time) will save eighteen.

5. At the beginning this must always go;
   To put it at the end would spoil the show.

6. Their ranks a chief in a new cloak o'erthrew;
   Their losses, clearly, were not less than two.

7. Something that looks as if it would require
   To be pronounced over your Christmas fire.

LXVII

QUINTUPLE ACROSTIC IN LATIN
(The lights are not one-word lights.)

UPRIGHTS

A, B, C, D, and *E.* Five Roman goddesses.

LIGHTS

1. Live peaceably (but you will have to thaw a bit first).
2. Crawl on the left (reversed).
3. With bounteous lap.
4. I am blessed with incense.
5. Mayst thou be absent from Asia.

LXVIII

Uprights

A. Once, with their martial name, they used to go
Carrying London's millions to and fro.
B. While daily pilgrims from the country-side
Often in this were fain to take a ride.

Lights

1. The eatables now almost gone,
This we can still fall back upon.
2. This light you'll find in an MS;
A Latin month you've got to guess.
3. Home of a Saint; its name, to tell the truth,
Suggests that kindly it would foster youth.
4. A curious title see
Of Indian monarchy.
5. Old English Christian name; if it had got an
Extra initial, you would think it rotten.
6. If the Zoo were for a joy-ride through the streets of
London hauled,
After what old-fashioned weapon might the vehicle be
called?
7. What searchings of heart have been caused by this light,
As to whether it ought to be "very" or "right"!
8. At Assouan a dam made we,
But lower down there's just a D.
9. A danger long ago to ships at sea,
But now it saves them from catastrophe.

LXIX

UPRIGHTS

Not quite an island A,
Not quite a town is B:
Each of them, you may say,
Close to England's Southern sea;
In either case the name
Is very much the same.

LIGHTS

1. Something which you may
Fish, or take, or play.

2. She heard a maiden sing
"The year is at the spring."

3. A European sculptor, who
His birth from Gallia drew.

4. Of wool a certain weight—
So dictionaries state.

5. What aviators do,
And what they do it to.

6. In Latin, strange to say,
Does not mean "send away."

7. A savor, such as you'd
Perceive in cooking food.

8. Be careful not to miss
The final light. It's this.

LXX

QUADRUPLE ACROSTIC
(The lights are not necessarily one-word lights.)

UPRIGHTS

Four methods of travel
You here will unravel,
In order of time;
Two and Four you can rhyme.

LIGHTS

1. Not at all! This advice you must shun,
   And join the three words into one.

2. A note before it and a note behind it,
   And in a flower you'll be prepared to find it.

3. *Per ardua* when you strive
   Where hope you to arrive?

4. When Worcester was the see of Bishop Gore,
   Tell me, what was the signature he bore?

5. A sub-lieutenant of Chassoores I sing,
   Who only loved his Mahree and his King.

LXXI

UPRIGHTS

A and *B*. Two great poets of antiquity.

LIGHTS

1. A plant that may quite easily be guessed;
   One letter at each end, and—and the rest.

2. A complicated knot to be untied,
   But there's a pointed instrument inside.

3. This part of your house should be easy to find—
   One letter comes first, and the rest is behind.

4. By the world's verdict (oft has it been fooled!)
   Fit for a ruler, if he had not ruled.

5. With this weapon dangerous
   His anger armed Archilochus.

6. It's nothing, when you play at ball,
   Elsewhere, the greatest thing of all.

LXXII

QUADRUPLE ACROSTIC
(The lights are not necessarily one-word lights.)

UPRIGHTS

A. This place was imagined of old
A curious assortment to hold,
B. A diner whose greed was controlled,
C. And a stone which eternally rolled,
D. And a very vile woman who sold
Her husband for enemy gold.

LIGHTS

1. Add spices (various)
And salt and pepper thus.
2. This gentleman has lost his head—his lands,
No doubt, have fallen into Cromwell's hands.
3. More frenzied still! This light
Is topsy-turvy quite.
4. So you must take the half-past three?
Well, well, we will not carp
At Fate's command: the car must be
Round at . . .
5. Now for a swim, and then a good sun-bath,
And then walk home along . . .
6. My lady's favor now shall I assay,
With this my hated . . . ?
7. Those last three lights, I must admit,
This epithet will nicely fit.
Sit further up to your end, Ralph.
My goodness! Is this . . . ?

LXXIII

UPRIGHTS

A and *B*. Blest pair! Collaborate's what you did—
Or should we say that you colluded?

LIGHTS

1. Too oft does the Englishman's home
   This gentleman's castle become.

2. And oft are the praises rehearsed
   Of one on this mountain who cursed.

3. She, surely, will afford a clue,
   This tangled maze to guide you through.

4. Letters with this inscription oft I've sent,
   Nor ever found their treatment different.

5. This system America repels,
   Though it's used almost everywhere else.

6. She understood its nature, for her mate
   Endured a Covent Garden porter's fate.

7. I'm sure you won't find this
   Next light, because it is—

8. "A royal beast; and yet he doesn't rule—
   Quite the reverse," says Tommy, fresh from school.

LXXIV

UPRIGHTS

A. A fish-like flower.
B. And when that name you get,
   Where's t'other upright? Find 'em in your net.

LIGHTS

1. Observe this always, wheresoe'er you go:
   (If you pluck out its heart, a heart 'twill show).

2. You must give him a grant,
   Or travel he can't.

3. He said, "I hunt for haddock's eyes
      Among the heather bright"—
   What fish would less have caused surprised
      To our old friend the Knight?

4. "Toil, envy, want, the *garret*, and the gaol"—
   What rival version twists the rich man's tail?

5. An Eastern river—cockneys might produce
   Much the same noise as very mild abuse.

6. Paint it? Why, yes: but carve it? Greeks say no.
   Ay, there's the rub—across a stream you go.

7. A bishop this often professes—
   We're hoping that this he possesses.

8. Snug little place, o'er the sundering tide.
   "Oh, is it really?" the house-hunter cried.

9. This coveted description doesn't *look*
   As if it argued value in a book.

10. I'm not in foreign parts; I leave not home,
    And yet you'll find me easily in Rome.

LXXV

UPRIGHTS

A. Half of it's built for the tide; Half of it's built
for the shore:
We'd much better shelter inside, For I fancy it's
going to pour.
B. Half of it's built for the shore, Half of it's built for the
tide;
And to live in it *can* be a bore If there isn't good
weather outside.

LIGHTS

1. Western ancestors cried to the rich for S,—
Its Eastern equivalent here you must guess.

2. This town must be grandly supplied,
Since it's got its own liquor inside.

3. A hybrid god of Orient tradition;
But here you must neglect the repetition.

4. Said to have "raised a mortal to the skies"
With instrument well tuned for telling lies.

5. This underfoot you're accustomed to wear,
But see how it suddenly shoots in the air!

6. Run! We mustn't miss it!—There!
It's gone without us, I declare!

7. Only two thousand you will need; that's lots
To anglicize this word, which is broad Scots.

8. Rightwards, downwards, rightwards—that's what you
must do;
Upwards, rightwards, upwards—interweave the two

9. There is a tide in the affairs of men
That only journalists can turn back again.

LXXVI

Uprights

A and *B*. He stood, one foot on either shore:
He does not stand there any more.

Lights

1. A name recalling controversial heat,
   Or mathematics, or a sad defeat.
2. Skaters, of the hole beware—
   There's nothing left to skate on there.
3. It may be black or red,
   Threatening, mute, or dead.
4. This bird, it can be said,
   Appears to have no head.
5. A quarter of a City famed,
   After an exclamation named.
6. With oil anointed here is seen
   A prince without in red and green.
7. Two letters not put in
   Make the defiled our kin.
8. Far from the madding crowd take Number Six;
   To make a fight, a prefix now suffix.

LXXVII

UPRIGHTS

A. Bill Sykes (writes Calverley) ran unawares
   Into my whole; my first crashed down, and there's
   No doubt he did my second down the stairs.
B. My first flies, shrilly shrieking, to and fro;
   My second o'er his enemies can crow;
   My whole has feathers white—so now you know.

LIGHTS

1. Day is bright,
   Dark is night.
2. In the singular, yes, it brings peace;
   In the plural, makes troubles increase.
3. Here you take, with little toil,
   A bottle from a kind of soil.
4. I must confess this light
   Is the reverse of right.
5. Old-fashioned garment, that by itself looks incomplete;
   Reversed, you often see them at your feet.
6. Reverse of Number Ten below—
   I mean the shortened form, you know,
   Beneath the sea it's wont to grow.
7. This is, or was, a kind of stern decree—
   If I can help it, not pronounced by me.
8. Into French you must translate
   Number Nine as Number Eight.
9. Reverse a discoverer—two letters add:
   You'll find you've got something that makes the heart
      glad.
10. From stronghold of the Huguenots delete
    A hapless maid who, riding, lost her seat.
11. Eight persons, since the weather seemed amiss,
    Did this upon the second half of this.

LXXVIII

TRIPLE ACROSTIC

Uprights

A, B, and *C.* Three operettas by a nineteenth-century
team.

Lights

1. I hope that this you haven't got—
   It is a more than orphaned pot.
2. This without effort you will find—
   The cult of heathen human kind.
3. Nothing could nobler be
   Than this word, obviously.
4. A tree, an insect, and one letter more
   Make up a Libyan tribe the English tamed by war.
5. May intercept a thief, or may
   Help him to get the swag away.
6. From habit very rude
   Most countries do exclude.
7. Reverse a verb which officers may fear
   (Or noun that keeps a pen behind his ear).
8. Daughter to memory dear—
   Had sisters eight, I hear.

LXXIX

UPRIGHTS

A and *B.* Two styles of architecture
I want you to conjecture.

LIGHTS

1. "Buxom and blithe and . . . " something more,
   But not on air as heretofore.

2. So many secrets it must hide,
   Pity it should have beer inside.

3. Title in Shakespeare, carrying little weight—
   Not much above six pound, I calculate.

4. Crash! Bang!
   Clash! Clang!

5. Sticks to you, but it doesn't mean
   Relapsing into ways unclean.

6. I pray, yet I preach not—
   An anagram of REACH NOT.

7. Hard is the passage of the needle's eye:
   This is the thing to pass through cities by.

8. A railway-station; letters come to it
   From every quarter of the compass (wit!).

9. Two forms of an alien genitive we
   In the name of this innocent heroine see;
   Omitted the name of an island must be.

LXXX

UPRIGHTS

A and *B*. The full description of a kind of bird;
  Each of the uprights is a single word.

LIGHTS

1. A certain town in England has this name;
   It looks as if it meant to make a claim.

2. Read it this way and that, this ancient state
   Must (one would think) have been effeminate.

3. Reverse this charlatan (who made a scoop),
   Prefix two letters—larger than a troop.

LXXXI

UPRIGHTS

A. Strange one should call it this, although it take
Such tons of stone the edifice to make!
B. How can it? Only solids, I feel sure,
This simple operation can endure.

LIGHTS

1. Sprite, that has many a kindly service planned
(By methods, naturally, underhand).
2. Where's the point? To the right?
Significant, quite!
3. If it be empty, you must drop
More: if it be.
4. With his alliterative comrade, he
Raided England in some early century.
5. This sound goes on unheeded all the day,
Yet has a warning which it fain would say.
6. Less frequent sound, whose harsh monotony
Has varied only once in history.
7. A writer: only change the D to E,
And all five vowels in the name you'll see.
8. A class so vague, description it defies;
A lighthouse what it is exemplifies.
9. Easy you'll find it; after slight reflection
You'll find with tea-sets it has no connection.
10. St. Bernard's pious monks, no doubt, this light
Could (when they found it there) translate at sight.

LXXXII

Uprights

A. Another name for Upright Number Two.
B. Alas, says Faustus, were it only true!

Lights

1. Two sticky things combine, and what one sees is
   An ancient form of Scripture exegesis.
2. To banish someone from a place of learning—
   Strange banishment, that homeward means returning!
3. Point of disembarkation for a ship
   Which made a long humanitarian trip.
4. When you have reached this light, you'll have some fun—
   Wholly correct solution there is none!
5. Long its brave walls an alien siege defied;
   But then, you see, it had a gun inside.
6. The hills so named in England you will find,
   Adding a tenuous luster to mankind.
7. Old orator: less egotistic, he
   A justly famed philosopher might be.
8. A common word, whose syllables are two
   And don't contain A, E, I, O, or U.
9. From 2 above take 14 lower down
   (Under another name) and leave a clown.
10. Two exclamations easily unite
    To form a nurse whose color isn't white.
11. Is this a vegetable? 'Tis a moot
    Point, for some people class it as a fruit.
12. A river huge: an added effort here
    Makes a much-needed quality appear.
13. Part of the head—put nothing on to it:
    Rather, that word itself you must omit.
14. Terrible goddess, who, with limping gait,
    Is bound to catch the sinner soon or late.

LXXXIII

UPRIGHTS

A and *B*. Daughter and mother.

LIGHTS

1. Imperial Lion we behead,
   And find a lizard there instead.
2. Attention, please!
   (It doesn't freeze.)
3. This word for idleness
   No term can well express.
4. This plant a rough portmanteau-word might seem
   For Hannibal's Italian-conquest scheme.
5. Dark is this light, without doubt;
   Behead it to find a way out.
6. No doubt but this
   Is what it is.
7. Poor, but honest? I don't know—
   The honest part had better go.
8. Continuous course, though it implies a bend;
   Its second letter lost, it means an end.
9. One of three kings, the word implies—
   North of the Trent his kingdom lies.

LXXXIV

Uprights

Two Browning poems.

Lights

1. Take one from a letter, and two from it—
   This electrical unit you surely will hit.

2. A Major Prophet's father bore this name—
   Let's hope his character was not the same.

3. A goddess, fearful vengeance wreaking—
   Why not say this, instead of "Speaking!"

4. Graphic—suggests a nice
   Throw in a game of dice.

5. Gambit of the 20's dancing floor—
   A Cardinal would ask no more.

6. Nero's glass of emerald
   By these stars will be recalled.

7. Here is what some
   Would render thumb.

8. When to crab a thing you choose
   Here's the epithet to use.

9. Stiffness should mean;
   I go between.

LXXXV

UPRIGHTS

A, B, and *C.* Philosophers—at our despair
One wept, one laughed, one didn't care.

LIGHTS

1. This Christian name suggests precipitancy
   (As her surname suggests loquacity).

2. This is a simple light, whate'er
   It would be, but what isn't there.

3. Cuts an odd figure—penniless this time,
   And for an unsexed girl affords a rhyme.

4. How dangerous must his pet have seemed at first!
   The cord about his middle is reversed.

5. When winter comes, the hearth's enough for me,
   But a large field in summer mine must be.

6. Did French but use portmanteau words, no doubt
   This is the way Shrove Tuesday would work out.

7. Only twelve have been crowned,
   And here they go the wrong way round.

8. Residence (but the final letter's missed)
   Of one who said he'd got a little list.

9. This vulture's head and tail are like in kind,
   But in the middle—there's the rub, you'll find.

10. Synagogue-ruler (badly hit)
    First you must find, and then omit.

LXXXVI

UPRIGHTS

A. Half of it's a beast, half is a machine:
   Put the two together—Lord, how long it's been!
B. Half is a machine, half of it's a beast:
   Put the two together—the milkman won't be
      pleased.

LIGHTS

1. This little English town accords
   To married love rewards.

2. This maid resolved to live her life reversed
   (Insert EN before her own name first).

3. In beast this quality,
   Not in machines, ranks high.

4. He slay us? This unworldly king?
   Banish the vain imagining!

5. In an imprudent moment, he
   Advised the English just to wait and see.

6. Queen of the place where sage and hero sit
   Silent, while horror grim broods over it.

7. Behead the word, and you will see
   What carried one (not recently).

8. Subject I'd much
   Rather not touch.

LXXXVII

UPRIGHTS

A. Drafty and dark experience forms a bird.
B. Cheap English beer might from this ancient garment
   be inferred.

LIGHTS

1. Simple, unaffected, yes—
   And yet half seems a doubt to express.

2. A notable traitor, yet he
   Stops short of sedition, you'll see.

3. In this cigarette, not a Turk,
   A snake unsuspected doth lurk.

4. This part of the body divide
   And you'll see there's another inside.

5. Nonsense behead, and reckless it will be:
   Then you behead again and find a tree.

6. Compel by fear
   Is fruitless here.

7. Sleep and race—
   It wipes your face.

8. To break off her engagement if she'd the intention
   What place on the Thames would a young lady
      mention?

9. A lyric poet's lady-love: add P
   And find a home of entomology.

10. Legitimate, yet dreaded
    As soon as it's beheaded.

11. Belongs to a strict vegetarian sect,
    So the rat in his middle you'd hardly expect.

LXXXVIII

UPRIGHTS

A and *B*. This is secret, that public; this serious, that
fun;
There are boxes for each— you can guess
Number One.

LIGHTS

1. This gentleman (swarthy, it would appear)
   Can never enter the forbidden sphere.
2. According to circumstance, this may be made
   Of beef or of mutton, of business or trade.
3. Goes in front, when it can,
   Yet it's ne'er in the van.
4. How it gambols and frisks! If you cut off its tail,
   To think of a prophet you hardly can fail.
5. Name of a mountain sung about by her
   Who played an Abyssinian dulcimer.
6. A kind of weapon guess
   That brings forgetfulness.
7. Speaker in England who wouldn't speak—
   In history, quite unique.
8. Stupid, quite,
   Yet more than right.
9. For one who shirks his duty, name absurd!
   "False nephew" would have been a better word.

LXXXIX

UPRIGHTS

A and *B*. I don't see who *could* have understood them,
Except the designers who planned them.

LIGHTS

1. A man should not (like this one) be
   Too fond of scents and hosiery.

2. This beast (if any such exist)
   Has been to the chiropodist,

3. And if it put *this* on to keep it warm,
   Not quite a rhyme, but very near, 'twould form.

4. Curtail that last, and make its head its tail—
   To find a number you can scarcely fail.

5. This little stream
   Unhindered doth seem.

6. Which one of the patriarchs lay
   Like an ass 'twixt two bundles of hay?

7. Now, several times repeat his name; you'll find
   That something sweet it will recall to mind.

8. And if on this last point you can't decide,
   A simple remedy should be applied.

XC

UPRIGHTS

A. A country strange; two-fifths of it might read
As an encouragement to spur your steed.

B. Strange horsemen here
From the same sphere.

LIGHTS

1. It's drawn continually
And wasted frequently.

2. A style of art, which (by its sound) supposes
A miracle more weird than that of Moses.

3. A kind of demonstration; I should say
The household god had better come away.

4. This covering suggests that fruit
May, after all, from thistles shoot.

5. Something—the name for that which came
Between the something and the name.

6. Sharpens itself. You wouldn't try
To reverse that light? Nor I.

7. Here, in the moment of defeat,
Silence perhaps is most discreet.

8. A measure small, but better (you'll agree)
Than if you should omit the letter G.

9. A land few travelers visit:
Reversed, it is—what is it?

10. Total this implies
Violent demise.

XCI

QUADRUPLE ACROSTIC

UPRIGHTS

A and *B*. An English informer.
C and *D*. The people who believed him.

LIGHTS

1. Part of an English South Coast port, reversed.

2. Italian in Italian.

3. To tickle, without its last two letters.

4. Scentless.[1]

5. The process of stopping a flow of blood with
   astringents, reversed.[1]

   [1] The last two words are not to be found in dictionaries, but
   they are perfectly formed English words, easily arrived at.

XCII

Uprights

A and *B*. Nature to science must her secrets tell,
Nor may thin vapors unrecorded swell.

Lights

1. Moab, thy king from Russian battle's reft,
   Nor aught is found but glowing ashes left.
2. A Moor in Shakespeare who, with brooding mind,
   Had shut the gates of mercy on mankind.
3. Familiar word to all who ply the loom,
   And yet on soldiers' lips a voice of doom.
4. "Like some proud column, though alone," stood Pitt:
   Gone is the arch, and the patrician split.
5. Those seas have many an isle for beauty famed,
   But this alone is from its beauty named.
6. Forty looked down, said Boney—you'd believe
   Grace only such a conquest could achieve.
7. Far from rich halls, of Parian marble made,
   The poor man rests content with headless spade.
8. "A strange experience once," the club bore said,
   "I had"— his yawning friend said *this*, and fled.
9. Here dwelt a man, whose charity's renown
   Has, in his name, immortalized the town.
10. Headless or tailless doth this light appear;
    Or head or tail must be abolished here.
11. This Eastern city tyrants ruled of old,
    And battened, doubtless, on their subjects' gold.
12. In this quotation (so the author hints)
    He's not responsible for some misprints.

XCIII

UPRIGHTS

A and *B*. You've seen their portraits in the daily Press;
Yet neither is quite daily. Can't you guess?

LIGHTS

1. A court musician, of whose demonstration
   The monarch showed but poor appreciation.

2. Strangely she put her sons to nurse,
   And yet she might have done much worse.

3. Ascend it cannot, nor descend,
   And looks the same from either end.

4. Whene'er you talk of bean or pea,
   This upon your lips must be.

5. What term would cockney speech apply
   To Pecksniff's insincerity?

XCIV

UPRIGHTS

A and *B*. Two characters in a play of Shakespeare.

LIGHTS

1. This ancient general drew the sword—but then
   Part of his name suggests the pen.

2. 'Twixt boxes it's compressed,
   And in its midst—a chest.

3. Two kinds of covering combine
   To form an animal malign.

4. Designed to release
   From peril of grease.

5. Respectability? Oh, well—
   One vowel changed, and it is hell.

6. "To go between"; an office must between
   First two and last two letters intervene.

7. Its first seven letters use two vowels twice,
   And but one consonant (occurring thrice).

XCV

UPRIGHTS

A and *B*. Fearless often this has sat
Near the dizzy heights of that.

LIGHTS

1. With the dull-headed J.P.
   Slender connection had he.

2. Ruined this town—no wonder, we may feel,
   It should have gone the round of Fortune's wheel!

3. Hence a poor maid was borne to depths below,
   And its reverse is also dead, you know.

4. The first installment paid upon a claim—
   In metaphor, a pillow so you'd name.

5. To the wedding he goes to look after the bride;
   Don't tell me you cannot see any inside.

6. When to this place one with his wife would trip,
   The outraged booking-clerk replied, "Pip-pip!"

7. He died by a fall from the roof to the floor,
   And the rest of them buried him under his oar.

8. A quite well-known formation underground,
   Named from the hills where it is chiefly found.

9. Diseased (in body and in mind) within,
   And yet it has a toughish sort of skin.

10. With only half this bird you here must cope—
    The half that isn't half an antelope.

11. Give a twist to the nickname a general bore
    By a changed preposition—a twist, nothing more.

XCVI

THE IRREDUCIBLE MINIMUM

UPRIGHTS

A and *B*. Spare
Fare. [Very English.]

LIGHTS

1. Constrictor.

2. Atrides.

3. Turk-victor.

4. Alcides.

5. Tutor-bear.

6. De'il-may-care.

7. Mal-de-mer.

XCVII

Uprights

Two of the world's great conquerors they—
One spelled in an unusual way.

Lights

1. We men (although it bids a reptile stay)
   Often upon this substance make our way.

2. This you will need to oil your car, that's clear,
   But let us have no pious unction here.

3. An oasis of palm-trees the wanderers faced:
   A short stage of their journey must here be retraced.

4. A king, in this his Eastern home,
   Decreed a stately pleasure-dome.

5. The solution here needed, you'll find, comprehends
   Every point of the compass between its two ends.

6. Connected with seafaring; and inside
   You'll find the town where a great Roman died.

7. By this a daily need's supplied;
   Its anagram is Centrified.

8. If to this process I should be
   Subjected, and a nation, we
   Should have got back to Number Three.

9. A town that's named propitiously
   To suit its English University.

XCVIII

UPRIGHTS

A and *B*. I must tell you the two uprights are the same,
 Combining (in a manner cabalistic)
The arrangement unconventional to name
 Of this acrostic (not to say acristic).

LIGHTS

1. This, surely, shouldn't floor you;
 The word is there before you.
2. It needs a lot to take him down, a lot
 To make him take you down (and blunder not).
3. When this word in the plural you've guessed
 It's a burden or two off your chest.
4. Here to himself from Number Nine omit—
 But little value you will get from it.
5. A steam-ship is this
 Or merely a hiss?
6. A fizzy drink we
 Or two centuries see.
7. A well-known coal-field you must guess,
 Distrained upon without success.
8. This city is the acrostician's friend—
 Its midst a harbor, nought at either end.
9. An early Greek grammarian he,
 And a life-saver, obviously.
10. It simply means the same
 Under another name.

XCIX

DESIGN FOR AN URN

UPRIGHTS

A and *B*. You'll find no words, of course,
But of all words the source.

LIGHTS

1. He thinks (that's why his name's so long)
   That to be Broad is to be wrong.
2. Give the Italian version, pray,
   Of sculpture which (in English) may
   Remind you of a thirsty day.
3. Both officers and men this feeling bore
   (And should bear still) who fought in the First World War.
4. Four times multiplied, reversed:
   (Make sure that pussy's in there first).
5. A man who writes letters; the pen he should wield,
   But a more lethal weapon you'll find he's concealed.
6. A playful spirit; it is rather rum
   That you don't change it if you leave out some.
7. To gaffer and to gammer by
   Common consent it will apply.
8. In Southern seas; Sir William Harcourt's heir
   Its latter half did as a nickname bear.
9. I hope you will not thus re-write
   The title of the eleventh light.
10. Part of the face, or (in a loose
    Sense) its unduly frequent use.
11. Here you only have to find
    The Scottish cleric of reforming mind.
12. Not thus, but frugally, let's try to live:
    (A light whose first three letters light will give).
13. In Bible page (Authorized Version, mind)
    I doubt if any longer name you'll find.

C

Uprights

A and *B*. Valedictory.

Lights

1. Here our . . . section we attain;

2. The yawning reader says " . . . ! That's done:"

3. His sentiments I . . . , being one

4. Who ne'er with pleasure . . . his brain.

5. 'Tis mine no more to . . . you of your sleep,

6. Taxing your . . . with wiles

7. And riddles, solving which at first . . . smiles,

8. But later . . . away, saying, " 'Twill keep."

9. So this last airy fabric . . . space

10. Fades, like the wrecks of some . . . tea,

11. Whence the . . . to the Schools must be

12. Returned, and . . . good time the Vicar face

13. . . . the bill for broken crockery.

INDEX OF UPRIGHTS (NUMERICAL)

(The lights will be found alphabetically arranged in the index which follows this, with reference marks to show which Acrostic each belongs to.)

1. Balaclava — Agincourt. **2.** Rudyard Kipling. **3.** Angles — Angels (St. Gregory and the British slaves). **4.** Assault — Battery. **5.** Business — Pleasure. **6.** Golconda — Eldorado. **7.** Decimal Coinage. **8.** Coldstream — Grenadiers. **9.** Pharaoh — Pyramid (the lights will be found to arrange themselves in pyramid formation when written out). **10.** Capulet — Orlando (in *As You Like It*). **11.** Hamlet — Alonso (in *The Tempest*). **12.** Marmalade — Breakfast. **13.** Musical Chairs — Kiss in the Ring. **14.** Drake — Blake. **15.** Hawke — Blake — Drake. **16.** Drake — Blake — Rooke — Hawke. **17.** Telegraph — Telescope — Telephone. **18.** Victoria — Waterloo. **19.** Grosvenor — Bunthorne (in *Patience*). **20.** Felix kept — On walking. **21.** Garrick — Burbage. **22.** Pembroke — Cardigan. (This is an April-fool Acrostic; Somerset and Cornwall will not do, because "Review" does not quite fit the words of the 5th light.) **23.** Rubric — Bishop. **24.** Czecho-Slovak. **25.** Queer Street — Fleet Street. **26.** Trafalgar — Gibraltar (Browning's *Home Thoughts from the Sea*). **27.** Haricot — Chariot. **28.** Property — Accident. **29.** Peel Fell. **30.** Quadruped — Tetrapody. **31.** Cornish Riviera. **32.** Lawn-tennis — Tennis-lawn. **33.** Pineapple — Artichoke ("Jerusalem" artichokes from *girasole*). **34.** Fahrenheit — Centigrade (each light in this Acrostic is a word of three letters). **35.** Aristotle — Alexander (the Issus). **36.** Crocodile — Alligator. **37.** Harlequin — Columbine — Pantaloon. **38.** "Since there's no help, come, let us kiss and part." **39.** Nymph — Naiad— Oread — Dryad. **40.** Caesar — Cicero — Brutus — Antony. **41.** Lamina — Animal (its reverse: so lights 4, 5, and 6 are the reverse of lights 1, 2, and 3 respectively). **42.** Addition — Division. **43.** Boswell — Johnson. **44.** Lycidas — Sabrina

— Harapha. **45.** Chilterns — Cotswolds. **46.** Wellington — Cheltenham — Haileybury. **47.** "A Sonnet is a *moment's monument*" (Rossetti); "In his hands the thing *became a trumpet*" (Wordsworth). **48.** Harbour-bar — Bar-parlour. **49.** Bannockburn — Preston-Pans. **50.** Jane Austen — Persuasion. **51.** Robin Hood — Friar Tuck. **52.** Æschylus — Sophocles — Euripides. **53.** Trollope — Meredith. **54.** Portia — Imogen — Olivia. **55.** Sackbut — Theorbo. **56.** Warwick — Wickwar. **57.** Coliseum — Alhambra. **58.** Saint Peter's — Westminster. **59.** Abracadabra (both sides). **60.** Garibaldi — Mussolini. **61.** Bezique — Old Maid. **62.** Promenade — Bandstand. **63.** Canterbury — Walsingham. **64.** Paradise — Regained — Pilgrim's — Progress. **65.** Card-table — Bath-chair. **66.** Sardine — Anchovy. **67.** Vesta — Venus — Pales — Ceres — Flora. **68.** Vanguards — Guard's van. **69.** Portland — Landport (lights 5 to 8 are the reverse of lights 1 to 4 respectively). **70.** Coach — Train — Motor — Plane. **71.** Virgil (or Vergil) — Horace. **72.** Tartarus — Tantalus — Sisyphus — Eriphyle. **73.** Beaumont — Fletcher. **74.** Delphinium — Mignonette ("find 'em in yer net" — Sorry!). **75.** Boat-house — House-boat. **76.** Colossus — Of Rhodes. **77.** Coal-scuttle — Shuttlecock. **78.** Pinafore — Iolanthe — Patience. **79.** Decorated — Byzantine. **80.** Hen — Emu. **81.** Lighthouse — Breakwater. **82.** Transmigration — Metempsychosis. **83.** Invention — Necessity. **84.** Abt Vogler — Pied Piper. **85.** Heraclitus — Democritus — Aristippus. **86.** Dog-watch — Watch-dog. **87.** Nightingale — Farthingale. **88.** The Ballot — The Ballet. **89.** Futurist — Pictures. **90.** Brobdignag — Houyhnhnms (*Gulliver's Travels*). **91.** Titus — Oates — Silly — Goats. **92.** Law of Charles — And Gay Lussac. **93.** Dilly — Dally. **94.** Horatio — Laertes. **95.** Steeple-jack — Weather-cock. **96.** Bath Bun — And Soda. **97.** Alexander — Timurleng. **98.** Criss-cross (each side). (If the lights are arranged according to their length, tapering in from both sides at the middle, the uprights will read criss-cross, if required; the whole being in the shape of an X.) **99.** The letters of the alphabet, in order, A–M and N–Z. (If written out according to the lengths of the words, the acrostic will assume an urn shape.) **100.** Cheerio, pip-pip — Good-bye, so long!

INDEX OF LIGHTS

A

A–A. Abana, **35**, 1; Abracadabra, **59**, 1, 4, 6, 8, 11; Abora (Coleridge's *Kubla Khan*), **88**, 5; Absis Asia, **67**, 5; Ad astra, **70**, 3; Aella, **3**, 1; (pod)Agra, **14**, 3; Alabama, **65**, 2; Alaska, **62**, 7; Allaha(bad), **12**, 7; Ammonia, **37**, 2; Ana(gram), **63**, 2; Anda(man), **48**, 2; Angora (William Watson's *A Study in Contrasts*), **26**, 8; Anthea(p), **87**, 9; Arethusa (Shelley), **26**, 5; Argentina, **54**, 6.

A–B. Agib (*Bab Ballads*), **26**, 3; Ahab (reversed, Baha), **4**, 1.

A–C. Ant-arc-tic, **33**, 5.

A–D. And, **42**, 1.

A–E. Antigone, **58**, 2; Ariadne (who gave Theseus the clue to the labyrinth), **73**, 3; Assassinate, **52**, 1; A-start-e, **50**, 2; Awe, **34**, 2.

A–G. Agag (reversed, "gaga"), **7**, 6; Aggreg(ate), **1**, 2; Always grog, **64**, 4.

A–H. Aleph (Codex Sinaiticus), **55**, 2; Amurath, **65**, 6; A shady path, **72**, 5; Asquith, **86**, 5; (p)(h)Aunch, **44**, 6; Autograph, **27**, 2; Ayah, **82**, 10.

A–I. Anti(pater) (first of the Herods), **56**, 2; Ashanti, **78**, 4; Asi(nine), **21**, 5; Assegai, **2**, 5.

A–K. Asterisk ('as to risk), **12**, 5.

A–L. (c)Abal, **60**, 6; Adel (suburb of Leeds), **41**, 6; Ariel (*The Tempest*), **11**, 2.

A–M. Annam (reversed, Manna = What is it?), **90**, 9; Anselm, **9**, 5.

A–N. Aaron (*Titus Andronicus*), **92**, 2; Agamemnon, **96**, 2; (n)Airn, **40**, 2; Alan (Breck Stewart, in *Kidnapped*), **41**, 2; Albion, **1**, 4; Annan (reversed, Nanna), **32**, 8; Antilatitudinarian, **99**, 1; Argon, **66**, 2; Arun, **40**, 5; Avilion (in Tennyson's *Morte d'Arthur*), **13**, 6.

A–O. Ado, **6**, 8; Ambo, **18**, 8; Amitto (to lose), **69**, 6;

Antonio (*Merchant of Venice*), **17**, 7; Ar-mad-ill-o, **95**, 9.

A–P. (st)Amp, **84**, 1.

A–R. Adder, **12**, 2; Alder (Irene, in *A Scandal in Bohemia*), **15**, 2; A free cigar, **64**, 2; Air, **49**, 2; Ajar (reversed, Raja), **13**, 10; Anger (reversed, Regna = kingdoms), **8**, 9; A-nswe-r, **97**, 5; Antimacassar, **94**, 4; Arar, **9**, 3; Arthur (in *King John*), **10**, 2; (c)Avalier, **72**, 2.

A–S. An-droc-les, **85**, 4; Arquebus, **68**, 6.

A–T. Adam-ant, **30**, 3; Anchoret, **79**, 6; Ararat, **82**, 3; Asphalt, **97**, 1; A(u)nt, **1**, 9; Aut (reversed, Tua), **4**, 4.

A–U. Acu(men), **1**, 7; Adieu, **60**, 2; Adieu ('Ad you?), **92**, 8; Allu(vial), **77**, 3; Alu(minium), **48**, 9; Amu(let), **50**, 5; Anu(bis), **75**, 3; (m)Artiu(s) or (m)Aiu(s), **68**, 2.

A–W. (et)Aga-dooW (Wood-agate, reversed), **16**, 3.

B

B–A. Bala, **65**, 7; Boa, **96**, 1; Boadicea, **1**, 1.

B–B. Baa-lamb, **88**, 4; Bulb, **59**, 2, 9.

B–D. Bored (board), **22**, 4.

B–F. Bailiff, **73**, 1.

B–G. Brag (Garb reversed), **63**, 7; Bunting, **21**, 1.

B–H. Baksheesh, **75**, 1; Breath, **90**, 1.

B–I. Boli(via), **51**, 3; Buzi (father of Ezechiel), **84**, 2.

B–J. Benj(amin) (submitted to ex-amin-ation), **43**, 1.

B–O. Baloo (in the *Jungle Book*), **96**, 5; Baroko (a mood in logic), **60**, 5; Bassorilievo (bas-relief), **99**, 2; Beano (may there *be no* moaning at the bar), **48**, 8; B-ocard-o (at Oxford), **61**, 1.

B–P. Bac-up, **49**, 1; Bap, **5**,1; Bo-peep, **48**, 4; Boustrop(hedon) (an ancient style of writing, partly from right to left), **49**, 8.

B–R. Bunk-er, **55**, 5; Bursar, **21**, 4.

B–S. Brutus (*Julius Caesar*, I, 2), **23**, 3.

B–Y. Bur-berry, **90**, 4.

C

C–A. Ciherabara (Arabarchic reversed), **40**, 1; Cophetua (Tennyson), **36**, 1; Corona (cigars), **57**, 1; C-rime-a, **56**, 6.

C–B. Club, **65**, 1.

C–C. C.C., **98**, 6; Cabalistic, **98**, 1; Citric, Critic, **1**, 5; Civic, **45**, 1; Critic, **59**, 5; Cuc(koo) (cf. Koodoo), **95**, 10.

D–T. Dot (= full stop), **69**, 8.

D–V. Dav(it), **42**, 3.

D–W. Dunmow (the Dunmow flitch), **86**, 1.

D–Y. Dog-berry (*Much Ado About Nothing*), **30**, 9.

E

E–A. Ecbatana, **92**, 11; Elmira, **22**, 2; Enna (whence Proserpine was carried off; reverse of Anne), **95**, 3; (s)Enorita, **38**, 2; Epiphania, **46**, 2; Era, **34**, 8; Era (reverse of Are), **32**, 2; Escholtzia, **47**, 4; Estremadura, **37**, 5.

E–B. Eliab (1 Sam. xvii. 13), **57**, 6.

E–D. Ed(dish), **30**, 8; Edmund (in *King Lear*), **10**, 6; Emerald, **62**, 9; England, **28**, 5; Euclid (a child learns billiards with cue reversed, i.e. with euc), **61**, 7; Exercised, **100**, 4.

E–E. Eagle (Keats on Chapman's *Homer*), **25**, 9; E-clips-e, **8**, 8; Elaine (Tennyson), **25**, 3; Elecampane, **83**, 4; Enc-ratite, **87**, 11; Engine, **88**, 3; Entente (NT intervening between the significant letters), **17**, 4; Epitome (Dryden's *Absalom and Achitophel*), **25**, 10; Ere-mite, **29**, 2; Essence (alluding to philosophical disquisitions on Essence and Existence), **17**, 2; Eugene (Southey on the Battle of Blenheim), **25**, 4; Euterpe, **78**, 8; Exe-crab-le, **84**, 8; Exegete, **16**, 5; Exercise, **33**, 9; Expletive, **15**, 5.

E–H. Eighth, **53**, 8.

E–I. Eli, **34**, 5; Emi(grant), **74**, 2; Ennui, **33**, 4; Epi(logue), **63**, 5; Eucli(dean), **20**, 7.

E–K. Earmark, **21**, 7; Emb-ark, **77**, 11.

E–L. Ebal (Deut. xi. 29), **73**, 2; Eggs-hell, **29**, 3; Eper aveal (reverse of Laeva repe), **67**, 2; Epinal (Belloc's *Path to Rome*), **61**, 2; Evil (Live reversed), **3**, 5.

E–M. Elam (reverse of Male), **80**, 2; Elim (reverse of Mile), **97**, 3.

E–N. Elim-ination, **97**, 8; Embon(point), **20**, 2; Euston (contains 3 letters of North, 3 of South, 3 of East, 3 of West), **79**, 8; Evan (Nave reversed), **58**, 7; Exertion, **22**, 8.

E–O. Ebro (reversed, Orbe), **50**, 9; Echo, **100**, 3; Elcho, **19**, 6; Embargo (reversed, O grab me), **7**, 2; Em-brog-lio (or Im- brog-lio), **71**, 2; E-rat-o, **45**, 6; Ergo (reversed, Ogre), **24**, 3.

E–P. Ethiop, **47**, 12.

E–R. Ebor (= York; reversed, Robe), **65**, 9; E'er, **85**, 2; El-gar, **36**, 9; Elpenor (end of *Odyssey*, X), **95**, 7; (sept)Ember, **35**, 9; E-pistol-ographer, **99**, 5; Excelsior (Longfellow), **81**, 10.

E–S. Egress, **43**, 5; Empedocles (his slipper found after his leaping into Etna), **62**, 5; Ere(bus), **14**, 5; Eros (in *Antony and Cleopatra*), **11**, 5; Est dessous, **64**, 8; Eucalyptus (= easily hidden in Greek), **50**, 4.

E–T. Ear-nest, **95**, 4; Edit (Tide reversed), **75**, 9; Encrust, **40**, 3; (s)Everest, **58**, 9; Ex-tin-ct, **12**, 9.

E–U. Esau, **5**, 6; Esrohnu (Unhorse, reversed), **5**, 6.

E–Y. Em-bass-y, **79**, 2; Eulogy (the Yule-log), **66**, 7.

F

F–A. Formosa (Latin), **92**, 5.

F–C. Fac(simile), **34**, 1.

F–E. Fence, **78**, 5.

F–O. Folio (reversed, "oil of"), **20**, 1.

F–P. Fop, **89**, 1.

F–R. Fever (Keats' *Ode to the Nightingale*), **26**, 4.

F–S. Frolic-some-ness, **99**, 6.

G

G–A. Galba, **71**, 4.

G–B. Gninrub ("burning" reversed), **46**, 7; Grub, **19**, 1.

G–C. Got-hic, **21**, 6.

G–E. Grate ("colon" for "coal on"), **81**, 3; Grouse, **6**, 1.

G–G. Go-ring, **87**, 8; Greg(ory), **3**, 3.

G–H. Gath (2 Sam. i. 20), **90**, 7.

G–I. Gemini, **84**, 6.

G–M. Gam (*Henry V*, end of Act IV), **60**, 1.

G–P. Glossop, **17**, 5.

G–R. G-asp-er, **87**, 3; Geikwar, **68**, 4.

G–S. Gules (*Hamlet*, II, 2, 479), **90**, 10.

G–T. Grandparent, **99**, 7; Grit, **86**, 3; Gaunt (*Richard III*), **26**, 7.

G–Y. Gypsy, **82**, 8.

H

H–A. Halma, **24**, 5; Hedda (Gabler), **85**, 1; Hegira, **31**, 7; Hermia (in *Midsummer Night's Dream*), **11**, 1; Horsa, **81**, 4.

H–B. Hub(bard), **48**, 1.
H–C. Hellenic, **27**, 1.
H–D. Hindhead, **9**, 7; Hubbard, **15**, 1; Hundred-ey'd, **39**, 5.
H–E. Harrogate, **80**, 1; Hecate (he-cat), **13**, 9; Hellebore, **17**,
　　9; Hongree (in the *Bab Ballads*), **70**, 5; Hose, **75**, 5.
H–G. Hedge-hog, **86**, 8.
H–H. Hash, **88**, 2.
H–L. Han-nib-al, **94**, 1; Hovel, **92**, 7.
H–N. Hen, **34**, 3.
H–O. Heigho, **100**, 2; Hoangho (O hang O!), **74**, 5;
　　Horatio, **45**, 2.
H–P. Hencoop, **37**, 1; Hop, **52**, 5; Hsactekcop (reverse of
　　Pocket-cash), **38**, 1.
H–R. Her, **34**, 7.
H–S. Hercules, **96**, 4.
H–T. H-ear-t, **87**, 4; Hot-ten-tot, **51**, 6.
H–U. Honolulu, **99**, 8.
H–W. Hee-haw, **81**, 6.
H–Y. Hoy(den), **9**, 2.

I

I–A. Idola(try), **78**, 2; Iguana, **5**, 4; Ilia (mother of Romulus
　　and Remus), **93**, 2; Ilva (= Elba), **51**, 4; Inca, **57**, 4;
　　Interamna, **44**, 4; I.R.A. (ira), **18**, 2; Irredenta, **20**, 4;
　　Isca(riot), **87**, 2.
I–C. Iambic (Horace, *Ars Poetica*), **71**, 5.
I–D. Ind, **34**, 9.
I–E. Ianthe (Landor), **35**, 3; Ingratitude, **46**, 5; In-sin-u-ate,
　　31, 5; In-terce-de, **94**, 6; Iron grille, **64**, 6.
I–I. Iberi (Arnold's *Scholar Gipsy*), **54**, 5; Illi(nois), **13**, 11;
　　Impi (not "pi"), **42**, 4; Incubi, **98**, 3; Indi(gent), **83**, 7;
　　Inti(mate), **60**, 9; Intimi(date), **87**, 6; Iri(descent), **42**, 6.
I–M. Ibidem, **61**, 4; Idem, **41**, 4.
I–N. In, **100**, 12; Ich-neum-on, **7**, 4; Icon (the controversy
　　as to pictures and statues, with reference to crossing the
　　Rubicon), **74**, 6; Iron (Nor I, reversed), **90**, 6; Isaurian
　　(Leo the), **83**, 1.
I–O. Im-brog-lio (or Em-brog-lio), **71**, 2; Incognito, **18**, 7;
　　Inigo, **23**, 5; Ino, **37**, 8; Into, **100**, 9; Intro(it), **66**, 5;
　　Italico, **91**, 2.

L–K. Lock, **33**, 8.

L–L. Labial (B's and P's), **93**, 4; Land-rail, **29**, 4; L-awful, **87**, 10; Lenthall (and the Five Members), **88**, 6; Lepadological, **17**, 3; Lethal, **88**, 7; Level, **93**, 3; Lobloll(y), **46**, 4; Lull (Gray's *Elegy*), **26**, 6.

L–N. Laban (Gen. xxix.; reversed, Nabal, 1 Sam. xxv.), **43**, 7; Lien (reversed, Neil), **32**, 7; Lincoln (Bishop of, in *King Henry VIII*), **10**, 5; Lion (in *Midsummer Night's Dream*), **11**, 4.

L–O. Leanto, **36**, 8; Lim-popo, **1**, 6; Loco(motive), **43**, 6.

L–P. Lisp, **84**, 7; Loop, **69**, 5.

L–R. Letter, **76**, 3; Liar (reversed, Rail), **4**, 6; L.M.S.R., **38**, 3.

L–S. Less, **92**, 10; Lias (Sail reversed), **45**, 4.

L–T. Left, **77**, 4; Lightfoot, **13**, 7; Lut(her), **37**, 4.

L–W. Luck-now, **20**, 3.

L–Y. Lux-uriously, **99**, 12.

M

M–A. Macedonia (Acts xvi.), **7**, 5; Malta, **12**, 4; Mariana (Tennyson), **47**, 7; Minnehaha, **57**, 8.

M–B. Mab (Milton's *L'Allegro*), **47**, 1; Momb(asa), **12**, 1.

M–C. M.C.C., **47**, 3; Metric, **73**, 5.

M–D. MD (= 1500), **63**, 4.

M–E. Me, **74**, 10.

M–I. Medi (in Daniel), **41**, 3.

M–K. Musk, **13**, 1.

M–M. Museum, **47**, 11.

M–O. Malvolio (*Twelfth Night*), **11**, 3.

M–P. Men-dip, **82**, 6.

M–R. Matador, **22**, 3.

M–S. Mo-lass-es, **8**, 10.

M–Y. Magnificently, **39**, 3.

M–Z. Mahershalalhashbaz (Isaiah viii.), **99**, 13.

N

N–A. Nala (reverse of Alan, above), **41**, 5; Nausea, **96**, 7; Nau-sea, **6**, 6; Nursia (birth-place of St. Benedict), **68**, 3.

N–D. Nod (reverse of Don), **45**, 8; Non-gold (the logical contradictory of the term "Gold"), **39**, 1.

N–E. None, **82**, 4; Not-able, **47**, 13; Not-ice, **83**, 2; No-vice,

74, 7; Nowhere, **73**, 7; Now-here, **49**, 3.

N–F. Na-ïf, **87**, 1.

N–G. Nag, **34**, 6.

N–I. Napoli, **31**, 4.

N–L. Nautical, **97**, 6; Noll (in Browning's *Cavalier Songs*), **63**, 3.

N–M. Nizam (of Hyd'rabad), **47**, 5.

N–N. Nap-kin, **87**, 7; Ninepin, **42**, 8; Nineteen, **50**, 10; No(g)gin, **90**, 8; Noon, **32**, 4; Northmen, **3**, 2; Norwegian, **37**, 9.

N–R. Nadir (containing Ida reversed), **47**, 9; Neither, **19**, 7; Nether, **50**, 3; Nidor, **69**, 7; Nonjuror, **51**, 5.

N–S. Naps (reverse of Span), **32**, 10; N-egress, **83**, 5; Negus, **49**, 4; Nemesis, **82**, 14; Ness, **5**, 5; Not-us, **49**, 11.

N–T. N-a-scent, **33**, 3; Nest, **58**, 4; Noblest, **78**, 3; Nougat, **62**, 6.

N–U. Nordau (reverse of (sq)Uadron), **80**, 3.

N–V. Nerv(ii), (Antony's speech in *Julius Caesar*), **66**, 6.

N–W. Now (reverse of Won), **32**, 3.

N–Y. Namby(-pamby), **46**, 10; Ney (reverse of Yen), **46**, 6; Norroy (King-at-arms), **83**, 9.

O

O-A. Ocarina, **48**, 5; Olalla (in Stevenson's *The Merry Men*; = All alo(ne) reversed), **86**, 2; Onomatopoea (sound of words representing the sense), **79**, 4; Orchestra, **94**, 2; Ottima (in Browning's *Pippa Passes*), **69**, 2; Ouida, **81**, 7.

O–B. Omnib(us), **75**, 6.

O–C. Orderic (biographer of St. Anselm), **28**, 3; Osric, **51**, 8.

O–E. Obtuse, **88**, 8; One, **100**, 7; Oriole, **47**, 2.

O–F. Orif(ice), **76**, 2.

O–G. Og(re), **36**, 5; Olig(arch) (Scott on Pitt and Nelson), **92**, 4; Orangoutang, **22**, 6.

O–H. Oath ("Do you understand the nature of an oath?"— *Old Punch*), **73**, 6; Olivebranch (cf. Ps. cxxvii.), **77**, 2; Ostrich, **76**, 4.

O–I. Occi(put), **82**, 13; Octroi, **31**, 2; O-pun-tii, **9**, 6; Ori(son), **53**, 6.

O–K. O.K., **24**, 6.

O–L. Oml, **54**, 2; Oriel, **6**, 2; (c)Orol(la), **70**, 2; Ouse-l, **36**, 3; Oval, **57**, 2.

O–N. Oban (reversed, Nabo = I will swim), **62**, 3; Obe-ron, **19**, 8; (expect) Oration, **78**, 6; Origen, **35**, 6; Ovation, **19**, 3.

O–O. Odo (Oh do), **42**, 7; Ontario, **27**, 6; O-port-o, **75**, 2; Oporto, **98**, 8; Otranto, **43**, 2.

O–P. One-step (cf. "Lead, Kindly Light"), **84**, 5.

O–R. Or, **18**, 5; Or(pen), **51**, 2; (b)Oar(d), **46**, 9; Oder, **8**, 2; O-least-er, **6**, 5; (h)Osier, **53**, 3.

O–S. Ovoviviparous, **94**, 7.

O–T. Ocelot, **47**, 8; Orbit, **83**, 8; Ornament, **49**, 5.

O–U. Occu(pier), **51**, 7; Ocu(lar), **90**, 3.

P

P–A. Panama, **33**, 1; Perdita, **28**, 1; Platæa (between Thebes and Athens), **39**, 4.

P–B. Pub(-lic being three-sevenths of "license"), **62**, 1.

P–C. Punic, **22**, 1.

P–F. Plain-tiff, **29**, 1.

P–G. Paying, **100**, 13.

P–H. Par-any-mph, **95**, 5; P-lint-h, **33**, 6.

P–I. Philippi, **58**, 6; Psichari, **28**, 4.

P–L. Parochial, **100**, 10; Pistol, **10**, 3; Pool, **69**, 1.

P–N. P-aster-n, **20**, 8; Patron (Johnson's *London, A Satire*), **74**, 4; Pumpkin (in the story of Cinderella), **17**, 8.

P–O. Philo(sophy), **54**, 1; Piano, **100**, 11; Potato, **33**, 7; Presto, **30**, 7.

P–P. Pp (in music), **9**, 1; Pip(kin), **78**, 1; Putrid pulp, **64**, 1.

P–S. Puts, **100**, 8.

P–T. Part (reversed, Trap), **53**, 7; Pest, **38**, 4.

Q

Q–A. Quag-ga, **61**, 5.

Q–F. Quaff (Browning's *Cavalier Songs*), **25**, 1.

Q–L. Quodlibetical, **37**, 6.

Q–T. Quo-it (as two words, Latin for "Whither goes it?"), **30**, 1.

R

R–A. Remora (contains Rome reversed), **30**, 5; Replica, **27**, 3; Rhoda (Fleming), **9**, 4; Rhoda (Acts xii.), **62**, 2; (wa)RloA(n), **16**, 2; Robbia, **63**, 9.

R–B. R-hub-arb, **23**, 1; Rob, **100**, 5.

R–C. Reihsac (Cashier reversed), **78**, 7; Republic, **66**, 3; (he)Retic, **56**, 3; Rheumatic, **28**, 2; Rustic (Ate = Nemesis), **82**, 9.

R–E. Rache (*A Study in Scarlet*), **58**, 10; Rathe, **12**, 3; Rep-tile, **94**, 3; Reverie (of Poor Susan, by Wordsworth), **53**, 2; Rope, **19**, 9; Runagate, **28**, 6; Rusticate, **82**, 2.

R–F. Ruff, **51**, 1.

R–G. Reading, **97**, 9.

R–H. Road-crash, **17**, 6; Rub-bish, **23**, 4.

R–I. Rabbi (Longfellow), **26**, 2; Renasni (Insaner reversed), **72**, 3; Revi(sion), **22**, 5; Rhomboi(d), **85**, 3; Roi, **54**, 3; Rosi(crucian), **8**, 7.

R–K. Rock, **2**, 1.

R–L. Rail, **14**, 2; Ratel, **48**, 7; Regal (reversed, Lager), **36**, 2; Repel (reversed, Leper), **45**, 7; Revel (reversed, Lever), **35**, 2; Roll, **18**, 6.

R–N. Rag-a-muffin, **13**, 12; Rama-dan, **49**, 10; Rebellion, **37**, 3; Resin (risen), **63**, 6; Re-sin, **79**, 5; Reuben, **2**, 6; Rodin, **69**, 3.

R–O. Rococo (Rock-cocoa), **90**, 2; Rum goal too, **64**, 3.

R–R. R-after, **71**, 3; Ranter (cf. John Peel), **21**, 3; Re(e)fer, **48**, 10; Reporter, **98**, 2; Reviewer, **59**, 3, 11; Reviver, **48**, 3; Rider (Byron's *Sennacherib*), **26**, 9; R-i-go-r, **84**, 9; River (1 *Henry IV*, III, 1), **25**, 8; Ruhr, **98**, 7.

R–S. Res(cue), **60**, 3; Ross (The Man of), **92**, 9.

R–T. Requiescat (Matthew Arnold), **25**, 5; Rot, **34**, 4.

R–U. Rivu(let), **89**, 5; Rousseau (cf. Crusoe). **19**, 2.

R–V. Rev., **68**, 7; Rev(isit), **31**, 3.

R–Y. Rival in the way, **72**, 6; Rosy (Tennyson), **40**, 6.

S

S–A. Saba (A bas, reversed), **4**, 2; Saga (A gas, reversed), **66**, 1; Sex-age-sima, **8**, 5; Sum-atra, **44**, 7; Swastika, **75**, 8.

S–C. Sic (as used in quotations), **92**, 12.

S–D. Salad(in), **76**, 6.

S–E. Saccharine, **89**, 7; Same, **5**, 8; Set-tee, **81**, 9; See-saw safe, **72**, 8; Some, **5**, 3; Sore (Eros reversed), **32**, 6.

S–G. Sea-king (seeking), **13**, 13.

S–H. Sab-bath, **43**, 3.

S–M. Sa-gun-tum, **82**, 5; Scum, **57**, 5.

S–N. Siren, **68**, 9.

S–O. Sinu largo, **67**, 3; Soho, **76**, 5; Spectro(scope), **40**, 4.

S–R. Sc-avenger, **31**, 6; Sitter (in cricket slang), **58**, 11; Slur, **5**, 7; Super(man), **52**, 3.

S–S. S.s., **98**, 5; Sala-mis, **76**, 8; Sans, **13**, 3; Sardius (without the R = Suidas reversed), **45**, 9; Saxons, **3**, 6; Seams-tress, **50**, 7; Sesostris, **52**, 9; Sinuous (Coleridge's *Kubla Khan*), **25**, 6; Sispyts, **91**, 5; Sos(then)es (Acts xviii. 17), **85**, 10; So-sibi-us, **98**, 9; Sous, **98**, 4; Steer amiss, **64**, 7; Synonymous, **98**, 10.

S–T. Solent (and In-solent), **19**, 4; Sort (Tros reversed), **4**, 3; Spat (Taps reversed), **77**, 5; Sunlight, **55**, 1.

S–W. See-saw, **58**, 1; Shallow (and Slender, Justices in *King Henry IV*), **95**, 1.

S–X. Sealing-wax, **35**, 4.

T

T–A. Tirra-lirra (Tennyson's *Lady of Shalott*), **35**, 5; Titilla(te), **91**, 3.

T–C. Tabac, **77**, 8; Toc(sin) (Cot reversed), **65**, 5; Tunic(on), **89**, 3.

T–D. Tancred, **96**, 3; Ted, **35**, 7; Tod, **69**, 4; Tussaud, **86**, 6; Tweed, **8**, 6.

T–E. Tadpole, **47**, 6; Telephone, **18**, 4; Tis-I-phone, **84**, 3; Toe, **34**, 10; To taste, **72**, 1; Tyre, **95**, 2.

T–G. Thingummy-jig, **20**, 9; Tropsog (reverse of Gosport), **91**, 1; Turning (*Henry V*, Prologue), **26**, 1.

T–H. Trash, **87**, 5.

T–I. Taxi (tack's eye), **79**, 7; Tibni (or Thebni), **50**, 8.

T–K. Tick, **81**, 5.

T–L. Tool (Loot reversed), **32**, 1.

T–M. Tar-gum, **82**, 1; Tram, **58**, 5; Tram (Mart reversed), **53**,1.

T–N. Titan, **28**, 7.

V

V–D. Vi-vi-d (two sixes), **84**, 4.
V–F. Vive pacif(ice), **67**, 1.
V–G. Veg(etables), **68**, 1.
V–H. Varnish ("the touch of a vanished hand"—Tennyson), **19**, 5; V-etc-h, **71**, 1.
V–N. Vacation, **83**, 3.
V–R. V.R. (for Victoria Regina), **1**, 8.
V–W. Vow, **18**, 1.

W

W–A. Wallachia, **15**, 3.
W–C. Wenc(e-sla-us), **86**, 4.
W–D. Worsted, **92**, 3.
W–H. Whitechurch, **46**, 1.
W–I. Woi? (reverse of I.O.W.), **32**, 9.
W–K. W-hel-k, **56**, 4.
W–N. Woman (*Hamlet*), **43**, 4.
W–W. Wick-low, **56**, 1.

X

X–L. XL, **20**, 5.
X–U. Xanadu (Coleridge's *Kubla Khan*), **97**, 4.

Y

Y–A. Yolanda (of Italy), **44**, 2.
Y–I. Yci (Icy reversed), **52**, 6.
Y–L. Yell, **2**, 4.
Y–M. Yam (reverse of May), **63**, 10.
Y–R. Yarr(ow), **39**, 2.
Y–T. Youngest, **28**, 8.
Y–Y. 'Ypocrisy, **93**, 5.

Z

Z–D. Zend, **61**, 3.
Z–L. Zangwill, **24**, 2.